The Senior Class: 100 Poets on Aging

The Senior Class
100 Poets on Aging

edited by Laurence Musgrove

ISBN: 978-1-962148-14-6
LOC: 2024946468
Editor: Laurence Musgrove

Lamar University Literary Press
Beaumont, TX

PREFACE

This anthology began as a graduate course assignment to give my students experience in literary editing and publishing. I distributed a call for submissions in the Fall of 2023, and after receiving more than 400 submissions from about 150 poets, in the Spring of 2024, my twelve students and I narrowed this project to 100 poems by 100 poets.

The call for submissions asked for work that explored in the special language of poetry the themes of aging, including issues related to eldercare, retirement, mortality, grief, gratitude, earned wisdom, senior living, spiritual reflection, and physical and mental decline, as well as changing dynamics in family relationships and marriage.

In terms of formal considerations, we were specifically interested in poems that demonstrated careful attention to the elements of shape, line, music, comparison, and balance, and especially how those choices contribute to the cooperative aesthetics of form and thought.

We also challenged poets to consider new choices they might make in audience and poetic form as they pertain to aspects of narrative perspective, shape, sound, repetition, and enjambment.

The poems in the pages that follow reflect beautifully all of these considerations in topic and form.

I want to especially thank my student assistant editors for their contributions in selecting these poems: John-Nathanael Caesar, Katie Carpenter, Grant Compton, Summer Flores, Rebecca Hargus, Beth Haymond, McKenzie Jones, Marilyn Krum, Kayla Pellar, Ebony Sago, Amanda Sanders, and Amanda Sturgeon.

I hope you find here voices that reward your attention and are friendly to your understanding of those in our senior class.

—Laurence Musgrove

RECENT POETRY FROM LAMAR UNIVERSITY LITERARY PRESS

Lisa Adams, *Xuai*
Walter Bargen, *Radiation Diary: Return to the Sea*
Christine Boldt, *In Every Tatter*
Devan Burton, *A Room for Us*
Jerry Bradley, *Collapsing into Possibility*
Mark Busby, *Through Our Times*
Julie Chappell, *Mad Habits of a Life*
Stan Crawford, *Resisting Gravity*
Glover Davis, *Academy of Dreams*
Wendy Dunmeyer, *My Grandmother's Last Letter*
Chris Ellery, *Elder Tree*
Kelly Ann Ellis, *The Hungry Ghost Diner*
Dede Fox, *On Wings of Silence*
Alan Gann, *That's Entertainment*
Larry Griffin, *Cedar Plums*
Lynn Hoggard, *First Light*
Michael Jennings, *Crossings: A Record of Travel*
Markham Johnson, *Dear Dreamland*
Betsy Joseph & Chip Dameron, *Relatively Speaking*
Jim McGarrah, *A Balancing Act*
J. Pittman McGehee, *Nod of Knowing*
David Meischen, *Caliche Road Poems*
Laurence Musgrove, *A Stranger's Heart*
Benjamin Myers, *The Family Book of Martyrs*
Janice Northerns, *Some Electric Hum*
Godspower Oboido, *Wandering Feet on Pebbled Shores*
Dave Oliphant, *Summing Up: Selected Poems*
Nathanael O'Reilly, *Landmarks*
Carol Coffee Reposa, *Sailing West*
Jan Seale, *Particulars*
Steven Schroeder, *the moon, not the finger, pointing*
C.W. Smith, *The Museum of Marriage*
Vincent Spina, *The Sumptuous Hills of Gulfport*
W.K. Stratton, *Betrayal Creek*
Ken Waldman, *Sports Page*
Loretta Diane Walker, *Ode to My Mother's Voice*
Dan Williams, *At the Gates, a Refuge of Milkweed and Sunflowers*
Jonas Zdanys, *The Angled Road*

For information on these and other Lamar University Literary
Press books go to www.Lamar.edu/literarypress

CONTENTS

Possibilities

ROBERT ALLEN

It is possible when my stroke took place
I was on my hands and knees in the bathroom,
wiping up the spill of the water bottle
which had dropped from my left hand. I could not
say why this hand, on which I had depended
all my life, now grasped at the empty air.
I wanted to explain but I could not.

It is possible when my stroke arrived
a bolt of lightning leaped across the decades
to zap my heart and show the gaping hole
where a solid wall was supposed to be,
the kind of deep betrayal of which I claimed
my body was simply incapable,
or else my whole life would have been a lie.

It is possible when my stroke congealed
a message was writ large inside my blood,
what some would describe as a wakeup call,
a sign that something powerful must change.
Many people would jump to the conclusion
its source was divine. An odd few might say
the universe was making love to me.

It is possible when my stroke appeared
I was wandering in and out of sleep
with a poem I had begun to write,
weighing the technique of using the facts
of one's life as material for verse,
reciting lines I had not entertained
in forty-six years, my memory scrolling

faster than any fingered key could go.
As history crept in, my mind aflame
compared my poem to those of the past.
I felt myself part of a long tradition
until I woke into a voice not mine,
whose unseemly sound I could not control.
What sense of self I had was nearly lost.

It is possible when a stroke crowns me
again, I will be nodding in the bathroom
at the remarkable length of my toenails
or I will fall upon my favorite path
while the mockingbird dive-bombs overhead
or I will lie in my bed like a baby,
wantonly naked for the undertaker.

It is possible when my next stroke happens
I will be a hundred and twelve years old,
and where the Battle of Hastings was fought
I will be a fully dressed reenactor,
swinging my broadsword at Norman invaders
in a millennial commemoration,
brazenly dying a fake hero's death.

Coda
LINDA ANGELO

in the end
after untold years
of passion, clashes, apologies,
wishes and withdrawal, this is it:
me by your side when you are too weak to rise,
a cool hand on your brow, a toenail
trim, a bowl of ice cream
to lift your spirits
absolution

I'm As Old As Turtles

SHELLEY ARMITAGE

The pills line up and what a choice:
Solaray's probiotic (Adult 50+)
Curcumin C3 Complex,
Algae Omega, of course, (all those 3's)
Chondroitin by itself (better for the kidney stones),
something called "Golden Revived"
—God knows what—recommended by
a similarly aging friend.

If I took them all at once—these pills—
I might get a glimpse of a holy drug cartel,
the stoned hereafter.
(Someone once thought I was praying
but it was only scoliosis.)
Instead they're staggered throughout the day
like my lurching walk,
my electrified nervy hips,
my bone on bone.

What I really would like,
and over the counter please,
is a tonic for a good fade-away—
jumpshot, that is. Mine best
at the top of the key, floating right,
airborne, flicked wrist away from the fray:
the kind that once stupefied opponents,
pharmaceuticals and all.
The kind that now exists only
in my melatonin dreams.

On Having a Body

CARL AUERBACH

Idries Shah defines a guru as anything
that teaches you what you need to know.
It can even be a stone, like the one
I stumbled over taking my morning walk
around the reservoir in Central Park,

and thinking about the concept of embodiment
in the philosophy of Maurice Merleau-Ponty.
That stone taught me that actual embodiment
requires attention to where my feet step
when I'm walking along a rock strewn bridle path.

My latest guru was the kidney stone
that I endured for a week of agonizing days
as it wended its tortuous way down through my ureter
to my bloated bladder and then down from there
to my urethra where I finally pissed it out.

The best that I could do until the stone's expulsion
was to muffle my nightly moans so that my wife could sleep,
and thank God for OxyContin which for me was better proof
of his (or her or their) existence than the scholastic logic
of Saint Anselm's ontological argument.

If a man screams in the forest with no one present
to hear that dreadful sound, is it really pain?
Fuck Bishop Berkeley, I've been there. It is.
Is a scream of pain merely overt behavior, as per Wittgenstein?
Fuck him too. I've been there. Trust me. It isn't.

They say the pain that kidney stones produce
is equaled only by the pain of childbirth,
but without childbirth's tangible rewards.
So though Merleau-Ponty showed me Descartes' error—
We grasp the world by body, not through thought—

my kidney stone taught me a deeper truth:
that the mind is ill-equipped for dealing
with the vicissitudes of a brittle aging body
subject to assaults inner and outer from which
OxyContin is more protection than philosophy.

Graphology

ALEX BARR

With each day that passes I become
more like my dear departed father who
in life I never loved enough and now
haunts my handwriting
to make it look like his—
so small you need it magnified to read it.

Even if I shrank this print to share the feeling
you wouldn't see the loops and squiggles
curled like wire or twigs of beech trees
or flight of wrens or moths
that sprang from his humor,
struggle, stoicism,
and even the strangeness of his son.

The Flip Side

Back in the nineties, Leonard Cohen sang,
"I ache in the places, I used to play."

In my thirties, I loved the song
laughed full throated at the notion.

Forty years on I am the proud
owner of an enlarged prostate
and Cohen's *Tower of Song*
has morphed into a gothic fortress
with bad pipes in crumbling walls.

Doctors

JERRY BRADLEY

Sally studied to be a doctor
but had three children instead

I never wanted children
but have five doctors
none of whom I want

and they have children
and some of them do too

and they may also become doctors
but if none of us gets what he wants
why should they

yet they will have their lakehouses
and boats no matter what I say

and expect them to be paid for
by pounds of flesh, planks
taken from unworthy vessels

leaky and unsound
knees creaking and coming unbound

like old books
running short of words
having neither maidenhead nor mast

and on whose sinking prow I now stand
practicing these words, my last

An Old Man Sleeps

SHARON V. BROWN

What was he dreaming that night
when the shadow-maker crept to his bed
and stopped his breath mid-dream?

Was he thinking of that girl by the sea,
a lifetime ago,
who, tilting her head,
laughed a string of bright pearls
at his giddy banter,
then stopped his mouth with a kiss,
her fingers trailing a tender line
down his spine like surf along the shore,
       wild and uncertain?

Silver Alert
CAROL FLAKE CHAPMAN

Last seen speeding from the mall
Heading toward the delectable mountains

More accurately, ash blond alert
As she did not go gray willingly

Not her name but her number up in lights
Warning that a crazy granny is on the loose

Not so much raging against age as
Mustering a getaway from slow decline

She is on the lam, making a break
For what feels like freedom behind the wheel

It's not graceful, this aging business
Though some days she feels lithe as a ballerina

The horizons still beckon like the call
Of the wild and the distant drums

How do we get there when the desire
Is so much keener than the eyesight

The yearning never goes, nor the spirit
Nor even the hope, despite all odds

How do we know when it's time
What are the cues to leave the stage

To make room for the stand-in
To relinquish the spotlight

Even, at the last, to give up
The keys to the kingdom, or the car

I can still run a seven-minute mile, she says
But her knees, alas, tell a different story

Like an old racehorse she hears the call to the post
But her slight limp when she gallops is a giveaway

And yet, she says I'm not ready to go, not at all
Surely there is world enough and time

To invent a cure, to rescue a bird
To run for office, make a lasting mark

Maybe not save the earth, too late for that
But perhaps keep a corner of it untamed

In Sickness
Barbara Chilcote

The man can't find his keys.
The woman searches.

The man has a sweater
fraying at the cuff.
The woman mends it.

The woman
fills his pillbox, walks his dog,
buys him a special pillow
to keep his head upright
at night.

The man stumbles when he walks.
It's getting harder.

He tells her the speech therapist
says he's not as sharp
as last week.

He says he could live
for another ten years,
he feels better,
maybe they can go to France.

The woman
picks pastry flakes
from his gray and buttery beard.
It's possible, she says.
Maybe.

Hunger

PETER CHRISTENSEN

I want to tell you a secret
Before it is too late

it is the letting go
that heals us
before that moment
we hold the delusion
of anger in our brain
to fortify ourselves
against knowing
that to be right is worthless
although there is sometimes
a bit of vindication in it

I want to tell you a secret
Letting go sounds like

cut wings tearing the sky
open
feels like
the beak of a falcon
ripping open the breast
of a Robin
to divine its meat from the keel
the carcass of the Robin
is left by the falcon
resting on the top of the wall
where it was butchered
to be transformed
by the sun
into a dry husk
all that is left of knowing
is a few feathers
and the wind takes care of those

Weight Training
BARBARA CROOKER

> *and how can you train*
> *the body to be the body?*
> *—Carrie Addington, "Waist Training"*

How can I train this aging
body, with its baggage, the freight
load of dinners in France, plates
gleaming with sauce and cream, sauté
pans sizzling, a glass of rosé
at the start of the meal that's raised
to the setting sun? Breakfast: an array
of croissants in a basket, display
of *confitures*, especially les fraises
des bois, wild strawberries. I'm sedentary:
at my keyboard writing essays
or reading a roman à clef
cushioned in a chair. The days
when I ran before dawn, gone. Praise
be to my left knee; the right one says
"mercy" going downstairs. The pain in places
I never knew existed. Ahead, there's a station,
and I'm slowly chugging towards it. No weight
training at the gym or miles on the exercycle can stay
this decline. In the passenger car, a conductor sways,
pushing his clicker, punching tickets: sprays
of confetti, little o's litter the aisles, ricochet.

On My 75th Birthday

SHARON CUMBERLAND

I was standing at the window
painting my nails
when I heard a passing stranger
say—not "What is she dreaming?"
or "What lovely silver hair!" but
"Why does she bother?"

Or perhaps she was saying
"How is your mother?" or
"Where is my otter?" or
"Lend me a dollar." Maybe,
at my age, I'm getting hard of
eavesdropping.

I was standing at my window
looking at the moon
when I heard myself say
"Am I your daughter?" then
"What does it matter?" and then
"I still miss my mother."

Old Habits

JANELLE CURLIN-TAYLOR

The mind grows calm
Surveying an ordered room.

I long to see my mind this way:
A well-made bed,
Pillows fluffed, bolsters erect,
Coverlet smooth.

Surely such a mind
Writes measured verse
4 and 4 and 4 and...
No hanging participles.

Surely such a mind:
Always dusts before sweeping,
Sweeps before mopping,
Remembers names, birthdays, obligations.

A well-made bed
No wrinkled sheets
No lumpy blanket
No covers showing below the foot board.

Measured verse
Fluffed and erect
Evoking order, style, grace.
Dutch housewives scrubbing the sidewalks at dawn.

For Gene, Gone at 82

CHIP DAMERON

Your mornings miss you.
As do your friends.
I look out and take in the light.

I hear a crow calling out
your name. It flies off,
leaving the blue sky empty.

All scribbling now has ceased.
The earth absorbs an ending;
spring nears, brings new life.

Biking to the Green Burial Grounds
LORNE DANIEL

Still breathing
heavily, borderline

giddy, we pull off
sweaty helmets. A stand-on-the-pedals climb
up cemetery hill caught us a bit
by surprise—burning
quads and emptied lungs—though
we knew it was coming.

At woods' edge we stand
bikes, step into green
burial grove, rest
on a bench, contemplate the vigor
of bush and bees. This place
we have chosen to be wrapped in plain cloth
shrouds and lowered. Simply planted.

Odd, the vivid
energy today, flushing
through flesh that will slowly take its leave, abandon
our boneworks. Today our whole
being can sit a moment
in satisfaction, before we kick
our kickstands back. Today we savor
the return, the ride gently down and away.

Bedside Vigil
MARGO DAVIS

after André Kertész's Melancholic Tulip

At your bedside, a tulip wanes.
      Is it short on oxygen? Its papery

petals refuse to give in. Dare
      I mention its stamina? You fixate

on natural light like never before.
      Your round pasty face, dissolving

like Alka Seltzer. Has it come
      to this? All these years, a strong

constitution, I recall. Which is
      what I'm left with, recollections.

Tennis matches. A fallen souffle.
      Putting our Collie down. *Oh, look,*

Hon. Your drinking straw holds
      sentry above a riot of pill bottles.

Can you not hear me? *Here, suck*
      some ice chips. Your eyes follow

dust motes. *A sprite?* What can
      I possibly offer? That steady glance

pulls taut your chapped lips.
      You refuse a Vaseline-coated Q-tip.

The moon-faced wall clock
      snores softly during visiting hours.

Tabula rasa: white blanket pins
      bleached sheets that serve as a bib.

Nearby, a woman's *mea culpa.*
      A man objects to life support. And

whose will? Your ragged breath
      quivers, lifts, shakes free. You rest.

What Now Then

YSABEL DE LA ROSA

A silence forms new
walls within these rooms, a maze
defying passage.

      The blue shirt folded,
      the briefcase by the side door.
      When will you be home?

      This world without sense,
      the old refrigerator
      has outlasted you.

      Mold on the muffins
      you bought. What of the body
      now, those limbs I loved?

Without you, who am
I here? Have I not also
                died?

The Yard Sale

GERALDINE DELUCA

I heard a joke on the radio the other day
about a family that was holding what they called
their "Grandpa Finally Died" Yard Sale.

I tell my friends and they suck in their breath.
And yet, isn't it true?
There is the great outbreath of air
when someone old lets go.

My grandmother stopped taking her pills
when she was 95.
And still, she said, God didn't want her.
Her daughter, who was 75,
couldn't lift her anymore.
Then, as she approached her 103rd birthday,
God opened his arms.
And then at the mass,
the church played the Ode to Joy.

Are you kidding me, I thought?
And yet wasn't that what we were all
supposed to be praying for?

And then
there were the memories over a meal
the deep comfort of eating,
the murmuring and the laughter.

"Come on-a, now," she used to say.
And now, we all said, "Come on-a now."

There were the tears, and holding one another,
And then the putting on of coats and going home.

And in time, the sorting of old possessions,
A favorite photograph,
A pair of gloves,
Her rosary beads.

The shape of my eyes,
the color of my daughter's hair,
These genes, all our memories,
Remember when we were kids?
Remember the pots of macaroni?
Remember our childhoods?
Our lives?
All those years.
And now,
the yard sale.

Gerontion
STANLEY E. DENNY

> *Most of your reactions are echoes from the past.*
> *You do not really live in the present.*
> —*Gaelic proverb*

Gerontion, old man, you dance still,
as you have for your lifetime—
Then, the purpose was social
and you had choices: ballroom,
square, folk, line, and foxtrot.
(Too late for ragtime and jazz,
popular with an earlier generation.)
You cut your teeth on the day's
vogue that fit the music's pulse.
Those are not the dances *du jour*.
Yours is an ancient, un-rhythmed,
ecumenical dance all embrace, a
ballet that shapes, purifies, and
measures unsuccess in errors.
But you are still dancing in the
mist of being and I know why.
You dance, sensing your music
ended long ago yet, your dance
continues because you fear that
when you stop you will discern
the world is not one you know—
that a questing new world vibrates
to different instruments; mourning
rules that have become anechoic
and those of trusted *lucidus ordo*.

Whispering to Mnemosyne

WINSTON DERDEN

Patricia is teaching me how to die.
Her body is food for cancer.
Patricia is learning on the fly.

No panic, fear, or alibi,
her calm remains, devoid of a hereafter.
Patricia is teaching me how to die.

Winnowing conundrum and mystery,
her method is question and answer,
until Oxycontin grounds learning, on the fly.

When I ask how to help, a surprise reply:
"Be your silly, goofy self, sir."
Patricia is teaching me how to die.

Framing fearful symmetries
I catalog what's left to remember
of Patricia's teaching on the fly.

In hunger for the weightless mind,
she declines a last supper.
Patricia is teaching me how to die:
loose the burden of consciousness, learn to fly.

Damned Spring

JESSE DOIRON

Damn the spring. I am a winter man,
old and withered, ready now to fall.
All the sap has dried inside of me, and
the only green I show is vile bile that
seeps and oozes slow out of my holes.
I see no reason for the sky to smile,
or breezy airy clouds, or rain to puddle,
or birds to wander their ways back.
Butterflies and fireflies try my soul.
Squirrels fucking in the trees disturb.
Buds bounding out of stems confound.
The yard grows fast its fat sweet grass,
and the neighbors walk in the morning,
calling out "Hello" and "How are you?"
Some stop to talk to me so cheerily of
nothing more important than the day—
the beautiful, rising, sun-filled day,
with its faint, lingering scent of oxygen,
and the laughter of children at play,
and someone's dog barking far away,
and bicycles spinning quietly by with
healthy and happy and handsome
women, whose fulsome breasts roll
over their firm pink forearms as they
glide themselves along the road that
bends so pleasantly in front of my house,
where they wave to me, always delightedly;
although, I'm all gone gray and grim and grave,
and I am damned unhappy that it's spring.

When I Was Young
JUDITH R. DUNCAN

when young and healthy I loved them all
strong, sweet, and savory, all young boys
loving a redhaired youth, pale eyes, and oh so tall

leather shoes, thick socks, hike a faster pace
dance, sing with an old-fashioned boy-toy
when young and healthy I loved them all

always searching for red hair and freckled face
kissing under a porchlight—me being coy
loving a fair-haired youth, blue eyes, and oh so tall

grown old, frail heart, hair of silver lace
I long for living and loving for joy
when young and healthy I loved them all

alone here, alone there, such a lonely place
dark dyed hair, blonde wig, what must I employ
loving a curly haired youth, dark eyes, and oh so tall

praying bedside for one final embrace at last
I fail to wake for morning glory
when young and healthy I loved them all
loving a redhaired youth, pale eyes, and oh so tall

Elderly Woman Rocking

WENDY DUNMEYER

In her walnut rocking chair she watches
twilight ripen into dawn her backward
forward swaying a glissade into the
dim blue hours past silhouettes sighing
whispering as they pirouette through swirling
twirling leaves the skitter skirring of her
memories a grande jete the leaping
gliding guides her back in time between their
gray illuminations and the morning
light she watches from her rocking chair

Frost

LISKEN VAN PELT DUS

Winter's coming. Most of the trees
   are bare and this morning for the first time
a heavy frost ghosted my car.

By the time I drove to the store
it had evaporated, but oh was the sky heavy
   over the cemetery on my way, bullet-gray.

And of course someone was being buried.
     It made me sad, seeing the lines of cars.

It's strange, isn't it, that we think of ourselves
     both as leaving and as being left,
   our bodies—*us*—giving up the ghost,
   letting it go, but also *us* the ghost, freed.

My friend Catherine took her husband's ashes
   on pilgrimage back to the places
   he had loved and left
     some in each spot, his *remains* remanded
   to the bits of earth that witnessed him.

Soppy, a bit, but it gets at the seeing
     and the being seen that is living.

The frost didn't disappear. It just turned into sky.

I still see you.
I wanted you to know.

Daughter Heaven Mountain
CHRIS ELLERY

To begin her yearly wellness exam,
Dolores is given three words
to remember, a test for dementia.

"Daughter." "Heaven." "Mountain."

Pulse oximeter. Blood pressure cuff.
Stethoscope sounding her torso
for the beat of her heart, the flow
of breath. "Have you recently fallen?"
Dr. Darby asks. "Do you have trouble
getting out of a chair? Trouble
with drooling? With swallowing?
Incontinence? Vision? Memory?"

Meanwhile, ageless Ni Zan,
the Yuan master, paints a perfect world
in her brain. In his signature way,
he uses only black ink and leaves
large swaths of the paper
untouched by the brush, suggesting
sky or mist or water.

               From nothing
there emerges a bamboo grove
on a riverbank, plums and orchids
and gangly pines, a hermit's hut
tucked away in the cleft of a distant range
to prove the existence of humans.

Dolores learned long ago
how Ni Zan, in his last years,
gave away all that he owned
to take up the life of a Daoist wanderer
in the Lake Tai region of his youth.

Now she is straightening her blouse
as her doctor explains
the alarming numbers in her blood,
her prognosis and options.
To the doctor her smile as she listens

is disconcerting. Yet she hears
and understands, clearly, even
as she follows the wanderer,
the strokes of his brush.

Ni Zan leads her across
a rugged stream, under gaunt trees
with an owl perched on one high limb,
past a grassy swell where a doe
and fawn are browsing, into
a vast blank space,
where his brush pauses.

She knows she must travel through
on her way
to the far mountains drifting
in nothingness
below the untouched sky,
a tall mother mountain maternally rising
above her brood of little mountains.

"And now for the test," Dr. Darby says,
noticing her far-away look.
"What are the words
that I gave you to remember?"

Half in a mystic dream she meets his eyes
with her inscrutable smile.

"Daughter. Heaven. Mountain."

Burnt Dust

KELLY ANN ELLIS

1.

In a junk store, I sort through stacks of photos—
wedding pictures, black and white, orchids gone gray.
The bride chose that bouquet, picked the lace, those gloves,
the garden gate or trellis, backdrop for this most auspicious day.
What is this stuff? Who keeps keepsakes? Impulses lost, paper
translucent, names faded or forgot. I have heard that fires begin
in dust. Did you know dust can burn? Yes. Burn the house down.

2.

In ashes of burnt dust, I tally the number of lovers who have died
these past four years. Five. Faintly I remember sweat and secretions.
How one taught me about Mozart; one clipped his nails to the quick
(the better to feel you with, my dear), brayed like a dying wildebeest
in his over-heated bed. The third had never heard of Thomas Hobbes,
said the social contract wasn't really a thing. The next crushed my now-
frail bones beneath the weight of his need. The last swept me away—
no hurricane, just dust, with just as much disdain. Such fuss! I recall
their beds, stale sheets, me—my encouraging murmurs, words unsaid:
a little to the left, please. Where did all those juices flow when they died,
which they did.

Time After Time

MAUREEN TOLMAN FLANNERY

Old lovers with time on their hands,
tenderness intact, interest hyperactive,
carry one another on to the next time.
Slack, blue veined bodies respond.

Touch navigates around scaly brown patches
that arise on blotched skin the way
backs of turtles emerge out of ponds.
Faster than the last thing she just said,

he can recall the swish of the skirt
she wore when he first saw her
come giggling out of that unfamiliar church
and wished his throat might find words.

Most nights he just needs to rest
in nothing more than the warmth
of her skin against his chest.
In reverie she can feel his urgent

stubbled cheek against her neck
that time he pressed her young hips
against the corn crib and pleaded.
Perhaps, on one snowy afternoon

when old passions call them back to bed—
she with her prolapse, he going flaccid,
they'll agree it's too much work
and decide to give up trying.

Tonight she just curls into his sleeping S,
lulled by familiar sounds of his night breathing,
cradles his soft member in her cupped hand
and wonders if the last time was the last time.

Questions
ELIZABETH N. FLORES

Mama Consuelo took another fall,
tripping over her cane in her kitchen,
on her ninety-third birthday,
after proudly serving cake to everyone.

Now, her third trip to the ER in as many months.
Diagnosis: a broken shinbone,
added to cruel dementia.

Mama Consuelo's eyes were fixed on her right arm
as the young Mexicana nurse struggled
to find a vein for the IV. She didn't ask
why her leg was twisted, or when she could go home,
or what she always asked young Mexicana nurses.

"Who are your parents? Maybe I know them."

What mattered only to Mama Consuelo was if *her* mother
knew where to find her.

"Does Mama know I'm here?"

Yes, her children assured her, hoping the lie would hold
and praying there would be no further questions much
harder to deflect such as

"Is Mama on her way to see me?"

Encouraged by her children, Mama Consuelo
redirected her attention to the young Mexicana nurse.

"Sweetie, why don't you try my other arm?
I don't want you to get in trouble with the doctor."

Touched by Mama Consuelo's gentle prodding,
the young Mexicana nurse replied, "Yes, ma'am."

Birthday
DEDE FOX

First present arrives
with a flash of lemon fluff.
Feathery tail juts
from dog's mouth,
a warning,
dropped on command.
Stick-legged, open-eyed,
a tiny bird, yellow and grey,
falls, lovely even in death.

Sitting sentry now, on the other side
of a glass door, pup watches as I scoop
the yellow warbler into a green bag,
thoughts roaming to other trowels
used by family and friends
to scatter dirt on coffins,
the last holdouts of their generation
lowered into raw graves,
as I number my days.

Luella
CYNTHIA READ GARDNER

Snow encircles this place.
At the end of the hall
Luella's dying.
Last week, she sat in a chair,
clots of bright plum settled on her chest like wounds.
Alarmed,
I called for a nurse.
"It's just her dessert," they tell me.

Now she's on her back, staring through me.
White-knuckled fingers grip the bedrails.
I pry them away to hold.

A plastic tag around her wrist, her name
in thin blue ink,
the thread of a ring swims
on her finger.

Microcosm

Elisa A. Garza

"How is it that we live
mindlessly from one moment to the next?"
—Dorianne Laux, "Breathe"

My world compacts
to house and treatments,
the bayou that I walk,
birds that arrive and depart.

My microscopic cancer
treads with me,
nesting in lymph nodes,
waxing in cycles,
like a tiny new galaxy
with fertile clumps of gas
birthing young bright suns.
They build microsystems,
living mindlessly
within my systems,
in the moment,
so unaware of my small
shortening life
as the boundary
of their minute expansions,
unaware that their growth
will be my end.

But, at my end,
I will shrink
even smaller, contract
into a black hole.
I will unmake
all those little worlds
in the crushing dark,
an everlasting night,
strong within me.

Wonderful Life
MATTHEW GRAHAM

The great tragedy of the movie *It's a Wonderful Life*
Is that George Bailey never gets to leave Bedford Falls.

Yes, we see the town as if George
Had never been born—Potterville, actually

A dangerously attractive place—sort of like
Times Square in the late 70's. And still,

The movie has a happy ending. Sort of.
Jimmy Stewart flew twenty bombing missions

Over Germany when the life expectancy
For a bomber crew was 8 to 12 flights.

After the war Stewart had aged 20 years
And was no longer leading man material.

He almost quit Hollywood and considered moving back
To Pennsylvania to run his father's hardware store.

It's a Wonderful Life was his comeback.
Yet, it's been recorded that Frank Capra

Pushed at Stewart's P.T.S.—as of then unacknowledged—
To get the scenes he needed of George's

Shocking backlashes against his wife,
His daughter and his uncle.

I left my own Bedford Falls
As soon as I could.

No one was counting on me there. There was
No guardian angel who needed wings.

I think of this sometimes while crossing a bridge—
How much I may have left behind,

And how much sadness there is in that, though I am probably
All the better because of it.

Prayer for My Aging Senses

Amy L. Greenspan

May my fingers—arthritic now—never forget
the trust in a toddler's grasp

May I recognize spring when a warbler sings,
when wind-song dances through sycamore leaves

May fresh-baked bread still smell like home,
rain still smell like fresh-baked earth

May I always be able to see distant hilltops,
the deep iridescence of damselfly wings

May I taste—till the end—the sweetness of lips
blessing mine with a goodnight kiss

Widow's Words Unspoken

JEAN HACKETT

When you flatlined, I slumped in the hospital chair,
my disappointment and sweaty thighs
supported by industrial-grade vinyl,
your waxy fingers twisted into my wrinkled palm.

How dare you desert me after sixty-odd years!
leaving me nothing but a funeral to plan
for a smattering of unfamiliar belonging to our son's friends,
and the new pastor, a young man with no Sunday morning memories
of you highlighting scripture from a third-row pew.

Why couldn't you have dropped dead twenty years ago?
I had prospects.

I might have returned to nursing,
assisting doctors as they corrected cleft palates
under a Honduran canopy of trailing vines and squawking macaws.

Or sailed from Seattle to Alaska with my sister
to watch blue-green icebergs shiver southward
slowly as women of a certain age,
their true depths hidden like underwater shipwrecks
they left behind.

I could have married Bob after Martha died.
So often, I've pictured the two of us
like Diane Keaton and Jack Nicholson,
fishing for trout in a snow-fed Colorado stream,
real-life stars of a late-in-life rom-com.

Instead, I suffered twenty-five years
watching you piddle your retirement away
at home—repairing broken radios, flipping channels,
or emailing distant cousins
to trace your family tree back to Adam and Eve.

Now Bob's got Alzheimer's, and my sister's gone,
as has my ability to navigate the wheeled walker across rooms
without knocking over stacks of your Elmer Kelton westerns,
and medicine bottles you left unscrewed,
spilling pills across the carpet

next to where I accidentally overturned the box of your ashes,
leaving me to contemplate the scattered remains of my life
until the maid comes next Thursday to vacuum.

the painting *woman and child on a balcony*
SISTER LOU ELLA HICKMAN

by berthe morisot, 1872

though young
she wears widow's weeds
a black silken mystery
shrouding her time since his funeral
but today
she leans forward on a black gated fence
with her child standing next to her
in ethereal white
they watch the river as it flows on ahead of them...
having paused during their walk
they linger...
his fence that protected her
also hemmed her in...
she and her child walk on...
as they leave
can you hear her breathe

Recollection

VINCENT HOSTAK

The dayroom smells of potpourri—
dead-headed roses, lavender,
      abraded flakes of orange peel,
      and parched coils of cinnamon.
All sorted in a scentless factory.

Crowded in a stoneware bowl,
cloistered from the reach of rain,
      petals embrace a dry calyx,
      rinds draw closer to the bark,
recalling when they were beautiful.

Shaving with the Ancestors
JARED HOUZE

I splash water across my face,
look into the mirror,
and see my father.

But not in the way you're already assuming.
Like I'm making the tired point
that those we try hardest not to become
are the very ones we resemble.

No, he's just there,
wiping the steam away with the palm of his hand,
brushing his teeth,
not even looking back at me.

I know this because in the pools of his eyes
I see the figure of his father,
in front of another mirror,
pinching a half-Windsor around his neck
with a cigarette dangling from his lips.

All the while looking at his father combing Vitalis oil
into his thinning hair and buckling his overalls.
Right before he catches a glimpse,
in the center of that shifty glass
the reflection of another,

gazing into the image of a man I do not recognize,
humming a melody I've never heard.
Who, in turn, dips his hands
into the face of his father
floating in a water basin.

Then there are more faces.
One in a pond, another in a lake,
until there is a river
carrying all of them and hundreds more
into some vast expanse of blue that disappears with the curve of
the earth.

Standing in a hall of mirrors,
staring into endless seas of reflection
I feel the warm lather on my skin, press the razor to my cheek,
and begin to shave.

Aging Painter
CAROLYN HOWE

I paint myself in whitewater rapids,
grab a branch when my kayak capsizes;
at dusk roast trout on the campfire stove,
watch constellations set   morning haze rise.

I paint my legs propped on deck railing,
dog's head on my leg after hiking all day;
across the valley   the mountains I long for
right there   when I need   their calm.

With my paints, cold-press block, and round 20 brush
I could be in Paris   Barcelona   Crete,
or perhaps   be a child again,
climbing the tree in my front yard.

      I create   magic   that transports me
      from this body unwilling   from resources slim,
      and now   as these shadow years
      grow dim

I feel the pull of
alizarin crimson   burnt sienna   ultramarine,
as if   ancients are calling me
to a red rock canyon   where maybe

      I lived in a hogan
      many lifetimes ago,
      as if   by returning
      I'll remember.

The Bird in the Pesunia Tree, and the Clock
SABA HUSAIN

January 21, 2024, Karachi. I wake up from a power nap on the u-shaped sectional in my parents' family room. Tick, tick, tick, tick. The day I must fly back always goes like this. We all fall asleep. They, at the other end of the couch. I keep still so not to disturb their nap. It reminds me of any given afternoon of childhood, mild winters, summers with ceiling fans, endless days, solid lull of youth. Outside, a tiny bird hops, and is happy in the branches of a pesunia tree. I raise my phone towards the direction of the window to capture its song, but the traffic on the street is loud even though this room is in the back and faces an inner courtyard. It's like the white noise of T.V., and they continue to sleep, next to each other, feet stretched out, heads elevated on plenty of plush pillows, breathing softly through open mouths. These are the two that held me. I hold on, as I did to another time when I was about six or seven, and their beauty captivated me. How many trips do I have left, before they fall asleep, just like they do now. The clock ticks. I scan the room, but don't know where the sound comes from.

That Night in the Davis Mountains
KATHRYN JONES

Do you remember that long road trip we made
to the Davis Mountains the year Hale-Bopp
streaked close to Earth and across the Texas sky?
The comet would not come this near again
for two thousand years. It was once in a lifetime.
Back then we'd never heard of Alzheimer's;
all of our memories lay ahead of us
like the craggy blue mountains on the horizon.

We drove for ten hours, pulled into the state park
north of Fort Davis, got our permit from the ranger,
pitched our little dome tent by a dry creek.
At dusk collared peccaries roamed the campground,
rustling dry grass with their hooves,
searching for food with their small tusks.
After setting our watches for 4:30 a.m.,
we crawled into the tent, anxious, waiting.

At the beep-beep-beep, we unzipped the tent,
bolted out, aimed our binoculars up at the heavens.
There it was, a fuzzy silver head with twin tails,
one blue, one white, visible with the naked eye
even in the moonlight. When I looked down,
I saw an even more astounding sight—
a herd of deer sleeping around our tent.
They looked up at us with wonder in their eyes.

Many years later, I am the keeper of memory.
Soon you will forget even that night in the Davis Mountains;
it will fade like an old photograph in an album.
But the images stay fixed in my mind—the blue-silver comet,
the glittering Texas sky, the deer sleeping next to us,
protected in the park, content in the peace of simply being,
not fearing the unknown, not afraid of forgetting
what it was like to remember.

Local Warming

LIBBY FALK JONES

At eighty years, my grandma felt the cold—
that mild October day, we'd rushed to her—
I watched my mother rub and rub her mother's
freezing hands, to work away the blue.
Then Mother, too, at sixty-six—to light
a sparkler her last New Year's Eve, she cloaked
herself against Louisiana chill.
Now my years outrunning hers, my fingers stiffen
as I write, I shiver under blankets,
seize my husband in the night—I know now
why the old cat, his last six months,
plunged headfirst beneath the bedclothes
to line my chest with trembling bony fur.

Relearning the Language

MILTON JORDAN

Evenings about dusk our neighbor
across the courtyard lights her window lamp
and early most mornings we see her switch
the window back to darkness, marking
another morning to begin a day
like yesterday was and tomorrow will be.

We will, before evening, ask of her health
and she of ours and if we walked the trail
or weather forced us inside to walk
the long hall across the third floor bridgeway
connecting her newer building to ours
in this center "Where Caring Is Contagious."

Although caring remains routine,
with overnight swiftness they've scrubbed
that long used catch phrase from on site signage,
rebranded transportation's vehicles
and reprinted all agency paper
"Where We Care for One Another"
leaving contagion on that scrapheap of words
no longer heard in polite company.

Palimpsests

BETSY JOSEPH

At this stage of life
we are palimpsests—
alterations made on our original selves,
not unlike old manuscripts with erasures
allowing another's writing to occupy the space
while still leaving traces of the first author's thoughts.

We stop to glance into mirrors now—
not to admire our reflection
but to search for traces of recognition
in that face which appeared in early photos,
comparing the faded expression
with the face that returns our gaze.

Waiting for MRIs

CAROL KANTER

Creased with age, not current worry,
two men sit apart,
heavy jackets unzipped.
Neither picks up a magazine.

The stouter one nods at the other's blue cap,
its World War II insignia.
South Pacific? Army or Navy? Oh, I was Navy.
Seven battles. Clear as yesterday.

A third man enters.
Turns out he was Navy back then, too.
A clerk calls for Slim as Stout barrels on,

A storm beached my LST at Okinawa.
I got blinded, flown home to heal.
At least we were clear
what we were fighting for. Not like now.
Folks in Washington used to know
how to do war. How to get us home.

They reconnoiter, waiting for the fall-out
here at Nuclear Medicine.

Connections with Life in Spite of Dementia
IRENE KELLER

In serene quietness
she shows pleasure, joy
watching motions of life
through her large window with a view:

she smiles
as birds race in mid-air
to see who arrives first
at her birdfeeder set for lunch or dinner;

she points
at cars of various hues
that travel up the hill
needing to turn left, right, then out of sight;

she notices
a pedestrian moving slow
as she carries in one hand
a grocery bag and a toddler's hand in the other;

she watches
slight sway of flowers
while a city deer tiptoes
through them, looking for a spot of his own.

* * * *

Silently engaged
in the rhythms of life
is what intrigues my mother now,

but makes me wonder
if in her dementia frame
what she sees today connects to her past:
> hummingbirds that flittered on the edge of her favorite red bowl,
> tours she and my father made in cars, always a different color,
> daily walks she took to and from the corner grocery store,
> city deer who rested under her backyard pine,
> her flowers and her children she nurtured.

* * * *

Memories, or not,
she finds pleasure
in her perpetual presence
of being connected with life in her own quiet way.

Don't Die In
TINA KELLEY

January

it's my birthday month
plus there's that smell of steam heat
the datebook's best page

February

not Valentine's Day!
organizing and mending
Joe died then, not you

March

still no leaves, so death
is a black bag rattling
on flooded branches

April

not near your birthday
loss doesn't fit with rebirth
too pretty for death

May

babyman's birthday,
my month to be most fertile
and play in the soil

June

I already have
enough reasons to cry with
weddings/commencements

July

two words: it is our
wedding anniversary
don't ruin it please

August

it's our vacation
and mourners need more structure
to get through their days

September

beginnings, not ends
heading off to school, not grave
red apple, not worm

October

too many zombies
on front stoops, tombstones on lawns,
skeletons in stores

November

I hate irony
Counting blessings near turkey
you didn't cook? No

December

Don't make me force out
hollyjolly cheer with red-
rimmed eyes nope can't won't

Therefore

no month is open,
you're flat out of options,
so just stick around

Old Ice

KAREN KILCUP

Toss those cubes in the sink—
that's old ice, my mother insists.
It's turning gray, has cracks
that fracture into jagged
edges, contains the gossip
of frozen fish and bagged
broccoli. It's seen and heard
a lot, been shouldered
aside by smooth blue blocks
used and resurrected
dozens of times. Old ice,
superfluous until nothing's
left, is easily discarded.

Metaphors in Disaster

KATE KINGSTON

while emptying the dishwasher, a stroke

I hear the crash at 7am,
his body sprawled on linoleum. I dial 911,
a void in the cell service. I try
to get him up, crane with a busted lever.

His body sprawled on linoleum. I dial 911,
sprint to the neighbor's, a road runner,
try to get him up, crane with a busted lever,
his tumble of hair, a Pandora's box.

I sprint to the neighbor's, a road runner,
flag down the ambulance,
his tumble of hair, a Pandora's box,
a steed with flashing red eyes.

Flag down the ambulance,
wait for the medic to dismount
his steed with flashing red eyes,
this cowboy on a white horse.

I wait for the medic to dismount,
for the nurse, a posse of healing hands.
A cowboy on a white horse
takes scans of his delirious heart.

The nurse, a posse of healing hands
slips him into the metal tube
takes scans of his delirious heart.
She loads him onto the flight-for-life,

slips him into the metal tube
a time machine headed north,
loads him onto the flight-for-life,
a mustang, bucking, bolting,

a time machine headed north
I'm lost inside the waiting room,
a mustang, bucking, bolting,
an arsenal of vending machines

lost inside the waiting room,
a void in the cell service,
an arsenal of vending machines.
I hear the crash at 7am.

The Mattress

CRAIG KINNEY

I think fondly of my new mattress,
a sure sign of decline. At sixty-five,
the mattress has become a thing
of utilitarian domestic tranquility,
arm's length from the things that
matter: my wife, the sleep machine,
the reading light, water in a lovely
blue glass. Nights, I sink into the
memory foam and remember earlier
years when a mattress evoked wild
and feverish possibilities
of what could be,
of what should be,
of what sometimes was.
But now, I recline comfortably like
a king, or read, waiting patiently for
the first dark light of a night's sleep.
And when I wake, if I rise quickly, I
get to see the cadaverous imprint
of my own mortality.

Wordless

LAURIE KOLP

Sometimes I swallow frothy thoughts
stuffed under tongue—no wisdom worth
effort allowed, wide notions birthed
in limbo. I forget whatnots,

whatchamacallits I once fought
hard to recall. Imperfect words
I sometimes swallow, frothy thoughts
stuff under tongue. No wisdom's worth

white-water rafting through distraught
memory loss. You once said the earth
was better with me in it, stirred
my affection in a squeaky cot.
Sometimes I swallow frothy thoughts.

After All
JIM LaVILLA-HAVELIN

he knows
or thinks
        he knows
or says
        he knows

how it all
turns
        out

he's seen King Lear enough times
            to get the gist
and Bonnie and Clyde
    though he does not expect to go out
    in a hail of bullets
        a blaze of glory

he's been to wakes
and funerals
carried a coffin
        an urn
                the burden
                of what
                he should
        have said
        and never did
        and now
        too late

he has even heard the angels singing
sappy songs from the sixties
with a straight face, and tears

        and he has put down
        two cats
            looking them in the eye
            as the shot goes in
            watching

            them leave even as their

bodies stay

and after
all
knowing, thinking, saying
isn't really about
measuring
      minutes, hours, days, weeks, months, years

probably not decades—it serves little to get greedy
      at this point

Sweet, Bitter, Bittersweet
Mary Makofske

"Feed me," he says, and opens his mouth like a bird,
though I am the fledgling who long ago took wing.
Now that his weakness has a reason and a name,
he hopes his demands will keep me duty-bound.

Though I am the fledgling who long ago took wing,
when the spoon scrapes the bowl and rises to his lips,
he knows his demands will keep me duty-bound.
But I can't sugarcoat my bitterness.

When the spoon scrapes the bowl and rises to his lips,
though I see my reflection swimming in his eyes,
I will not sugarcoat my bitterness.
The sweetness he craves can turn on his body now.

I saw my reflection swimming in his eyes
when he slid from his chair. I thought he was faking.
Blind to how sweetness can turn on his body now.
Only the doctor's chart could prove me mistaken.

When he slid from his chair, I thought he was faking,
as he thought my mother was when she held her heart.
No doctor's chart could prove him mistaken.
Turning to stone under stress is my greatest art.

He thought my mother faked when she held her heart,
as I hoped she did, believing she'd never leave me.
Turning to stone under stress is my greatest art.
Whose daughter am I, turning my face aside?

As I faked my hope, believing she'd never leave me,
I never spoke my love. There would be time for that.
Whose daughter am I, turning my face aside?
Is it true there is nothing that cannot be forgiven?

I never spoke my love. There would be time for that.
Now that his weakness has a reason and a name,
is it true there is nothing that cannot be forgiven?
"Feed me," he says, and opens his mouth like a bird.

Elemental Elegy
LYNN MARTIN

I return to wide sky, silvered driftwood,
clouds wild, unleashed, the self
turned loose into the essentials,
air, earth, fire, these waters
a blue beyond blue.

What cannot be decomposed—cadmium, mercy,
oxygen, soul, cobalt, love, gold.

Eucharistic bread and wine, the elements.

I remember second grade,
white chalk on a blackboard,
tracing a perfectly made small a,
round and round, elemental.

First principles—humility, generosity, compassion.

What can decompose—certain bodies, languages, sweet plants,
butterflies, memory, stars, even the heart.

Each time I've met death,
another galaxy opened
beyond the one I had known.

Elemental, before the beginning, what was given.
Elemental, what we have lost.

Shades of Grey

DON MATHIS

I like how the light misted your hair
in the moonglow through the blinds.
It shines as radiant as the future.
I know you think misty hair is a sign of age,
but age is just a number. Although I'm 72,
I've always been immature for my age.
Your hair does not reflect your stage in life.
There may be five stages of grief,
but there are seven stages of misty hair.
Stage I: Stop pulling out grey hairs.
This path leads to baldness.
Stage II: Call it silver, not grey.
Stage III: You may want to change shampoo or gel.
Some conditioners may be good for auburn hair,
but may make misty hair look drab.
Stage IV: Don't expect sympathy from your elders.
Stage V: Don't expect sympathy from your peers.
Those young fools will only ridicule you.
Stage VI: Know that even though there is snow in the roof,
there is a fire down below.
Stage VII: There are worse aspects to aging.
Many.
Worse.
Aching joints, failing eyesight, extruding teeth,
forgetfulness, diminished hearing, forgetfulness.
Stage Fright: All are indicators of pending death.
But all are indicators that you are alive.
Here.
Now.
Enjoy it while it lasts.
Enjoy it while you last.

I Never Saw Her Dance
JEAN MCARTHUR

Her sons had vanished once they were grown,
Like baby spiders drifting off in the wind,
Widowhood had left her all alone,
Retirement put her career to its end.

Lacking purpose and feeling very old,
After fifty years in her house and 'hood,
She moved away when her home was sold,
To a seniors complex as she felt she should.

And then she danced!
I never saw her dance but she said she did.
With people and hobbies she was entranced,
Of domestic shackles she was finally rid.

Marriage and motherhood had been a slog,
A prisoner of conscience and convention.
Not fond of children, husband, or dog,
Performed her duties without dissension.

Now she could relax and play silly games,
Line dancing, concerts, and a social whirl,
Singing old songs, learning new friends' names,
As happy as when she was a young girl.

The Ghosts
JANET MCCANN

Sometimes past midnight the dogs will pace,
whine and murmur, head for the back door

Stand there waiting. And I hear outside
yips, a bark, a scuffling at the door

And I let mine out, they run around
in jagged circles and then come in.

I stand at the door and hear my former dogs:
Lizzie wants a ball, Padre a bone,

Muck and Jill a pillow to tear up—
There are over twenty, a lifetime of dogs

I'm over 80 and always had two of them.
They aren't here to cause me grief,

just to say it's okay, we loved each other
and no love is ever lost, I should lie down

with my two breathing friends and be at peace.

*

Sometimes past midnight the dogs will bark,
their fur rising behind their ears,

their stance a challenge. At the front
I hear these figures who have names and dates

I've culled from websites, news reports.
I sought their lines down databanks, wanting

to find out who I am and where I came from.
And here they are, challenging, quarreling. They say

*Hey, we may share blood but you have never
known us and surely never loved us,*

so why do you bother us now?

A Glance in Her Direction
DAVID MEISCHEN

Zelma O'Reilly, 1893–1991

These moments on the porch swing
before a morning class. Swish of tires
on 21st Street, lone car horn, snippets of talk
and a burst of laughter. On the walk out front

Bicycle Annie—reed-thin, sunbaked, liver-spotted—
maneuvers around exposed tree roots,
fissures in the cement, her pace arthritic
among the very young who step around her.

Midday haircut at the Goodall Wooten—
shaving cream, talcum powder, clipper oil.
Outside, observed through hand-billed plate glass,
a figure carved by Giacometti leans her bicycle into the throng.

Sun-flecked picnic table at Les Amis.
Burger leftovers, longneck beer bottles.
A glance in Bicycle Annie's direction.
And back. A single beat of the second hand.

Once at a busy street corner, once when
the crosswalk signaled go, someone stepped
from the amorphous crush swarming the Drag
and moved to help her to the other side.

Bicycle Annie yanked free of the hand
that touched her arm. Get away! Let me be!
The voice was blunt, the gesture fierce.
She leaned back into her handle bars,

stepped down off the curb. One slow step—
another, another—through the crosswalk at 24th Street.
Lifting front wheel to the curb, she leaned,
stepped up, stepped again, back wheel following.

And down the wide sidewalk toward 23rd,
the press of students parting around her, flowing past
while Bicycle Annie inched forward—steel in her posture,
doing this one thing, walking her bicycle among us.

This is Me
KEVIN MILLER

waving, another traveler on his way
to the vanishing point, me soon away,

this curve of a line parallel another,
the pencil construct shows the eye

good bye. Grant me this moment
for apologies, find here no list

of sins, this is blanket coverage,
an umbrella policy for wrongs,

insurance of no market value.
What anxiety wrought may full

coverage soften and may scars
be stars like pin hole kisses

for miss deeds time softens
like tracks tracing my slow

improvement, immortality
itself has no chance

to wax over ungodly
blunders, a Guinness

and a good laugh
could fashion

a ribbon on
the toe

tag.

Song of Joy
TERRY JUDE MILLER

> *"This life is hard."*
> *—Ada Limon, "Overjoyed"*

What song do the fire-flared robins sing
when seasons chase them from Jack Rabbit Road?
Do they fly away with the scarlet of holly,
the sadness of hickory's bark ruin, the first star-fall
of snow? Birds are like the rest of us, swollen
with our sorrows, choked by memory's smoke,
and pursued by winter's unrelenting breath.
This life is hard, as Ada writes. Creatures blessed
with it are cursed with constant endings,
seasons, loved ones, the always open mouth
of our own demise. It is no trespass to wonder
into evergreen fields of yesterday and recall
fermented berries heavy on the bent boughs
of celebration as we sing our drunken song
loudly and joyously while darkness pulls its cart
behind us on our journey to everywhere.

Morning Dance
LOUISE MOISES

Beside the trees on the dew damp grass
the dancing women gather,
throw off aging aches and pains,
forget they are in their seventh or eighth decade.
Nearby, three young girls turn somersaults,
their lithe bodies curving in ways the women cannot.
A spotted dog chases a bright green ball,
thrown and retrieved again and again,
while the sunlight filters
through the branches of the Redwoods.

Along the trail, a stream meanders,
barely moist, waiting for winter's rain,
a duck bobs on the surface of the pond
surrounded by the scent of cedars.
A little one with curly hair pedals his tricycle
trying to out-race his father's steady steps,
while the women twirl and spin,
arms open to the powder blue sky,
and the sunlight filters
through the branches of the Redwoods.

Above, a vulture circles, then disappears.
Six robins pull worms from the turf.
The laughter of children on the swings
mixes with the hum of passing cars.
A fat city bus opens its doors and kneels
accepting two elderly travelers in wheelchairs.
An old man canes his way up the cement path,
stops to watch the women frolicking,
as the sunlight filters
through the branches of the Redwoods.

On the ground beneath their rust-red trunks,
a daisy, diameter of a dime, sparkles
like a bride, her petals touched by light,
delicate as a breath, more precious than a wedding vow.
Nearby, the women exert their last bit of energy
dancing and dancing on the green grass,
now raising their voices in exaltation
for this day, for feet to stomp and legs to kick,
and the sunlight filters
through the branches of the Redwoods.

Stray Thoughts on Aging

John Morgan

Fairbanks, Alaska

Is everything new about getting old? Spring
and the melting snow, friends dropping away—
they sift underground, or washed by the wind
they circle the earth. Their names like chalk on
a blackboard pose the daunting equation of loss.

Yesterday I biked past the old beer and gun club,
rechristened "Hogwarts," to the edge of the slough
where it joins the big river. No bridge for miles
but a flagpole with pennants to summon
a boat when somebody needs to cross.

These blustery afternoons, deceptive in their
beauty—bright hopes leading us on. Fish camp
and then a hundred empty miles to the range
where mountains like grandparents lounging
on hammocks span the horizon. Clouds

like winged lions—Assyrian. Is heaven open
for business on days like this? And cycling back,
a bull moose browsing the roadside willows
turns his head and stares. He's like that difficult cousin
you can't help liking despite his prickly ways.

Brain circuits, axon and synapse, maybe
we've got it all wrong, like those late night
sophomore sessions when a light went on
and suddenly everything changed. Are we
our physical bodies? Are we anything else?

If the body's a river distilling the years,
then a time-lapse camera could track this life,
recording the snowballing wisps of decay, sloughed
skin and hair, like mayflies flitting, having their day,
while the waistline spreads like a delta toward the sea.

It leaves a glow, a whisper, a caress. Remember
that dusty floor we slept on before we owned
a bed? "But why do they call it sleeping?" you said.
Still there's a pungence to this breeze, a whiff of bliss.
Is heaven open for business on days like this?

Confabulation
SUZANNE MORRIS

My friend lives in a
different place now.

The sun slants softly
through the window shades

bathing her room in
a hazy candle glow.

She sits in a chair
nearby her tidily-made bed,

showing off a small
bouquet of flowers

for her 80th birthday

and peering into
the camera

with the same wistful,
trying-to-be brave look

that I remember from
the first time I saw her,

an only child reeling from
her parents' divorce,

thrust into my junior high
seventh-grade class.

Then, her eyes held a clue
to uncertainty

about her immediate future;

now, they reflect
uncertainty

about her immediate past.

Of the present, though,
my friend is clear:

she is eighteen, not eighty.

Her parents are still married
to each other,

and they are always near,
watching over her.

On the Trail, Door County, September
WILDA MORRIS

Two years ago I would have clambered
down the uneven path to the rocky shore.
Five years ago I would have taken
the steepest trail to the water's edge.
Ten years ago, I would have climbed
over surf-wet rocks to a point
above the turbulent water,
sat for an hour absorbing the pulse
and warming sun.

Today I'm content on this wooden bench
two yards back from the drop-off,
looking for distant sails and short streaks
of brief whitecaps, watching the cormorant
with its long neck and beak feed in the shallows,
listening to the lullaby of the lake.

Mourning at the Kaldi Café

CAROL LOUISE MUNN

Yesterday at the Kaldi Café
the fruit of my loss was melon—

honeydew, cantaloupe, red water—
ripe bites I cut with a fork

as I told friends the
answer to my question

where are you now?
After lunch I found

old handkerchiefs
the color of melons

that I wear around
my hair today,

your mother's handkerchiefs
I thought I had lost

pull my thick hair
away from the damp

base of my neck
for whatever air

there is to cool
the heat of my first

summer without you—
today pale greens and tangerines,

thin lines the color of seeds,
soften my severity.

At night when I untie my hair
I braid your name inside each cross—

my plaits rest on each breast
like you used to do.

Moving Day

JANICE O'MAHONY

Sheets smooth as always,
hospital corners,
never a day untidy.
Not in labor, up all night,
in sickness and in health,
not when the baby died,
or the morning of his heart attack.
Not this day
when they drive her
to a small, pale room
and a narrow bed
they will not let her make.

No space there
for her portrait as bride,
crown of white roses,
cheeks tinted pink,
eyes bright and young,
oblivious.

Her kids will sort it out.
They may want the sheets
but not the stories.
They will take the portrait to Goodwill.
Someone might use the frame.
For now it hangs askew,
revealing unfaded wallpaper
no light had reached.

The Body Remembers
NATHANAEL O'REILLY

for Annemarie Ní Churreáin

The skull remembers seventeen stitches
the ear remembers the scalpel
the forehead remembers the clash
of hipbone and brow, blood gushing into eyes
the mouth remembers the dentist's tools,
the crunch and snap of teeth torn from gums
the neck remembers the puncturing
of the cyst, the stitching of the wound
the back remembers the surgeon's blade,
the excision of cancerous cells, the scraping
of the dermis, the cauterizing of the void, burning skin
the shoulder remembers the throwing of the ball,
the stretch and snap of ligament, the power of propulsion
the elbow remembers the clash of concrete
and bone, splintering and fragmentation
the middle finger remembers the pressure
of the pen between the thumb and index,
the formation of the callus
the shoulder-blades remember sheets
of sunburned skin peeling like ancient wallpaper
the spine remembers the herniated disc,
the inability to stand straight and tall
the abdomen remembers the hernia,
the surgeon's insertion of mesh
the scrotum remembers the vasectomy
the testicles remember the cricket ball,
the impact of speeding leather and cork
the quadriceps remember the burn
of the hill at the twenty-third mile
the knee remembers bitumen and gravel, blood and pus
the shin remembers the crunch of steel-capped boots
the calf remembers the cramp, turning to rock
the ankle remembers the twist and snap,
swelling like a pufferfish, green and purple
the sole remembers coral slicing skin,
burning summer beach car parks
the heel remembers blisters weeping inside new leather boots
the big toe remembers the canal's submerged barbed wire fence
the ball of the foot remembers launching the body, taking flight
to jump creeks, snatch rugby balls from the air, dunk basketballs,
clear the rocks at the base of the cliff on the continent's edge

Service

MICHAEL OWENS

Like watching from a deck chair on a transatlantic crossing
I see you there outside in the garden walking nowhere
and he is there beside you every step of the way

You stop to pick a tiny deceased flower and he stops
You wander off the walkway and he is there guiding you
You sit down and he silent sits beside you

I wish I was more like him, more tolerant of your limits
More anticipatory of your needs, more observant
But then again I have been with you seventy years

He tolerates everything and shows only love
He has better training than I in this sort of thing
I am at the end of life and he is only three

If I but had the devotion
of your service dog

Companion Animals
PETER PEREIRA

After my father died, my mother began to sleep
with a large teddy bear she could cuddle and tell her troubles to.

After a friend's wife passed, he took long drives
alone in the countryside, comforted

by the dove-like sound of a woman's voice
giving him perfect directions over his phone.

Some people will find a new pet after a spouse passes
and give it a secret name. Others will read books

their partner used to love, and in return receive
special messages to guide them through their day.

As my husband and I snuggle in for another night,
rubbing noses like sea lions in our many-pillowed dream chariot,

I try not to think about which of us
will fall asleep first—

or of what I, his slobbering Picasso-eyed pug,
would do without him, my faithful and alert Great Dane.

Creatures grown accustomed to each other's ways,
like a pair of old horses leaning together in a field.

You will always be accompanied, an owlish palm reader once told me,
years ago,
and I cried at the thought of it, not knowing why.

Vanishing Point

CELESTE PFISTER

A solar event is this aging:
sunspots erupt on my skin
sudden questions like solar flares
disturb me at 2 a.m.,
my mother's roadmap useless to me
with its indistinct terrain,
detours and dead ends,
unmarked gas stations.

Memories too heavy to carry
I wrap carefully in acid-free tissue,
store in waterproof, archival boxes
as if beside my grandmother's china—
blue rose buds in pale green sepals
crowded onto fragile white dishes and teacups—
which only ever existed as a wish
she couldn't bring on the boat
to America.

Random questions I am loathe to classify
as relevant or irrelevant
like floaters inside my eyes
drift into focus only to vanish
when I try to examine them closely.
I wait impatiently for answers to point the way
like cracks in a sidewalk
or the lines on the palm of my hand,
or like this stream of words
which came as a vision
that sailed by
blue on white,
then white on white,
then nothing.

slow dissolve

D. ELLIS PHELPS

my grandmother keeps
little white pellets
sweetener she calls *saccharin*
in a tiny green bottle
i love to hold
in my small hand

in my small hand—
little white pellets
i drop in black iced tea   watch
the tiny balls fall through
amber liquid   —consider
their slow dissolve

a slow dissolve we consider
as we sit for supper
at the green formica table
in her kitchen
we eat brown gravy
and white bread

with white bread
we sop the gravy up
we do not speak   we listen
—the hens cluck & coo
through the open window
in deep contentment

in deep contentment
we sit sopping
& the water cooler hums
from the back bedroom
where the singer sewing machine
sits   at rest

at rest now   this singer machine
its wide black peddle its lettered gold
will sew a dress for me
   pink lycra knit
—a pretty dress for graduation
under my grandmother's hands
under my grandmother's hands:

—the fly swatter's slap
—pin curls & a scarf for my hair
—moist lemon pound cake
—the last supper in ceramics
—gospel tunes in the living room

gospel tunes in the living room:
—music she played the last time i saw her
—lp's on a turntable   scratched & hissing
—sound on an eternal loop

my grandmother's memory
—a white pellet   dissolving

Holdfast

SYLVIA BYRNE POLLACK

The Velcro of my mind has lost
    its stickiness—the myriad
        small hooks and eyes don't grasp

conversations or what I've just read
    like they did years ago. But forgetting
        is not the problem—it's failing to see

the procession of miracles that stream
    by me and through me each day.
        Not a failure of memory but of attention—

not noting my knees aren't creaking today
    neglecting to savor each singular plump blueberry
        oblivious to the bees bumbling

in the oak leaf hydrangea by the back steps.
    Between what the bees and the wind
        scatter, our sidewalk becomes

a pollen-paved yellow brick road.
    I skip along, long-term memories intact,
        long cords anchor me to my past.

Memorial of Bone

KYLE POTVIN

A friend died last night, one today, a sign
of what is to come. I don't mean death, more
a solitary ghosting as I pour
each night—alone—my cold, light-bodied wine.

*

I walk into the lake, each step a stone
sharp as a wolf's fang. Friends, where are you now:
Suspended in this ashen air somehow?
Beneath my toes, memorial of bone?

*

A small animal, lungs full, water frail,
drowns herself in a tempting skim of seed.
Her nails click against the smooth wall of need,
unable to escape the brimming pail.

The years advance

DONNA PUCCIANI

more quickly now. How long
have we been married?
Too long, he replies,
the old-fashioned humor
getting as tired as we are.

Forty-seven years are lost
somewhere between ruby and gold,
with no distinguishing gemstone,
although one website says amethyst.
Should I buy him an amethyst ring?
lavender pajamas? A book with
purple prose?

Plants are the suggested theme.
As if we need a theme, after all this time!
I have always done the gardening,
he the dishes. For nearly five decades
I have presented him with acer,
viburnum, Korean pear and the ill-fated ash.
Some years the hydrangeas do well.
One year we lost the lilacs.

We are themeless, timeless, slipperful.
We breathe in huffs, snore in the chair,
shuffle our feet, feel the cold now.
Our chores become rituals, wordless
prayers to the ubiquitous routines
that tie us together like vines on a trellis.

We are violets, curled among the forget-me-nots.
We have bloomed. We prepare
to nod off, once and for all,
dead-heading each other and ourselves,
our wrinkled skin sagging
like the petals of a finished iris
set against an amethyst sky.

His Rubber Boots

ELENA LELIA RADULESCU

For three seasons
she postponed stepping in
the old garden shed;
too hot, too damp, too cold.
She even envisioned
newborn mice on a rag pile,
pink bellies exposed
like raw burn wounds,
the skin healing slowly.
　　　Then spring came.
The forsythia bush burst into
stars by her porch,
a sweet breeze drifted in
on the smell of wet earth.
　　　She opened
the door to the shed.
Light fell on a spade,
on a rake, on her husband's
old rubber boots waiting
for the warmth of his feet,
dry grass clippings
still stuck to the heels.
　　　She knelt
on the hard, concrete floor
yearning to talk to the boots
as if they were small children
left alone in the dark.
　　　Hush, hush.
I'm here now. I'm here.

Older but not Wiser
MINDY REED

We writers will not be silenced.
Older persons with stooped backs,
Drift through the door, usurpers of the space,
Some are pleasant, others curmudgeonly.

Prompts and timed writing result in sharing stories,
We never comment on what we share aloud,
Listen respectively, most lost in our own thoughts,
More venting and complaining than poetry.

A curious young man from Kosovo joins us,
Wordlessly, his eyes question our laments,
Our endless mourning of material objects,
Things that can be easily replaced.

He has seen so many bombed out buildings,
Homes, schools, hospitals destroyed by mortars.
He does not know how to weep for our losses,
Our chipped teacups and stalled car motors.

Older does not always mean wiser,
It's about perspective, memories become distorted,
Suffering and loss are not a competition sport,
Grief is real, age robs us of more than youth.

doing battle
EVE RIFKAH

an apple a day keeps the doctor away
macs, courtlands, the rare macoun
she polishes on her shirts, dresses, skirts
to shine a shine of stars
apples baked with brown sugar, cinnamon, ginger
made into sauce with cranberries
to bring the rosy blush she wants to paint
onto his pale cheek
and chicken soup,
the butcher knows her feverish
pursuit of fowl
to cook with carrots and onions
studded in cloves like a Christmas orange
she will try anything
to keep the angel of death away

the clerk in the produce stand
no longer blinks when she asks
for garlic by the pound
at home her fist pounds hard the wide flat blade of the knife
smashes white flesh from papery skin
she maniacally chops garlic into everything
soups, sautés, sandwiches sprinkled in sugar
garlic to seek out the devil of disease
send him packing

she rubs her hands in rosemary
smooths her scented fingers over his face
through the limp strands of his hair
tries to tip the seesaw
burdened with pain
shift the balance across to pleasure

she reads all the herbal lore
seeks plants in fields and nature stores
fights this battle of possession

the bowl on the table
laden with the voluptuous curve of fruit
the round plumpness of health
that has long melted from his bones
the bowl she fills anew each day

At the Cardiac Clinic

DARBY RILEY

My old doc for my old heart
checks the pulse on my foot. Pulse
is good, he says. Blood work OK.
I'll keep you alive to 90.
(This seems unlikely since he's
10 years older than I am).
I reply that'll be great
as long as I keep my brains.
He says an esteemed colleague
went cuckoo at 85.
The catch, we agree, is once
the mind goes, you can't end things.
He puts two fingers to his
old head and pulls the trigger.
I say, no, doc, that's messy,
just swallow a bunch of pills.
His assistant frowns. We laugh.

Winter
LEE ROBINSON

Haven't you been lost
to yourself
looking out the window
without seeing

until the old elm
blooms with birds
its dark limbs
alive with them

and your heart stirs,
you see what the tree
has been trying to tell you
about living

Look
how it bends with the wind
who comes this day
for a little ballet

See how the waxwings
in their elegant
everyday costumes
delight it

how it doesn't waste
its precious time
craving a finer landscape
with a better view

or quarreling with death
which is no enemy
but was there in the seed
from the beginning

Haven't you been
too long looking for home
as if it were somewhere
not here, not now?

And as for happiness,
that fickle temptress,
let the old tree tell you
what you already know:

how to be alone,
how to wait
for the company of waxwings
and how to let them go.

Waking
EDWIN ROMOND

I needed three alarm clocks
to wake up mornings in my 20's,
each set five minutes apart
to finally yank me from sleep
and greet another day of being young.
There was no space then between
dreams and the buzz of alarms.

But these days I wake on my own
long before I need to and just lie
there as sun erases the night.
Sometimes past people and places
appear like a sad memory slide show
and I try but can't reach back to sleep
to escape what I've done or

haven't done, people I have loved
and those I had hoped would love me.
Why do they wait until the first hint
of a new day to drag me back
to what I long to leave behind? Why
do some sorrows remain like stains
upon the heart, wounds that wait

for sleep to unleash at dawn? So
I rise early to shave yesterday's stubble,
seek a shower's absolution before
going downstairs for the comfort
of coffee then turn on the news
of other people's lives and forget
for a while the scars that remain in mine.

No Parts Spared

SHEILA RONSEN

It's insidious this breakdown
of my body, a body
I'm no longer supposed to identify with
but I can't "Ohm" my way out

of my degenerating discs pressing on nerves,
or my stiffening knees as I climb stairs—
each step a station on a Via Dolorosa.
Elevators have entered my prayers:

Bless Elisha Otis, May he rest in peace.
I'm undergoing an internal skeletal remodeling
where a super abundance of osteoclasts
are eating up my osteoblasts like Pac-Man.

It's too late to refuse renovation.
I'm left with bone grief, a diminution
of stature, fears of fracture. Faith
in my bodily resilience grows brittle.

I see my future crafted of spare parts:
titanium hip sockets, cobalt-chromium knees—
a cyborg that alarms the airport metal detectors.
I am hazardous material.

The blood of my beloved tomatoes
turns into an acid trip
transcending my stomach
flowing upstream into my esophagus.
The heart burns with what must be renounced.

Senior Singles

GARY S. ROSIN

After you reach a certain age,
what you want in a man changes.
A man who can drive after dark,
that's all you really need, she said,
but it helps if he can stand
at your side at openings,
chat with your friends about art,
listen to poetry readings,
then drive you back home, but slowly,
so you can watch the world go by—
no need to speed into the dark.

Support
JOHN RUTHERFORD

He asks for help so gently
and I never tell him no,
walked him to class on Thursday
because he couldn't go alone.

Watched him log into the computer,
he's done it a hundred times before,
but today he's down and wanted
just a little more support.

After, he asked me about Neruda,
if I'd ever read his work,
began to quote one on love,
hid his stammer with a smirk.

Locked his keys in his office (again),
but that's not even all that weird,
everybody does it once but he's
nearly brought to tears.

I watch him struggle and apologize,
ask if there's anything he needs,
but he smiles as his ride turns up,
gets in the car, and leaves.

Playing the Flute after Long Absence

JAN SEALE

The silver is the first to hear the tone
and then the lip decides it too can like
the mellowness that slices like a knife
the silent air on which the note is blown.
The player feels the burden all alone
to shine the tarnished piping back to life.
Strangely, as the notes pile to the light,
the tune, like water, seeks its own.
The fingers gain a temporary cure
from arthritis, dull procrastination;
the embouchure minds its reputation.
Sculptured sound recalls it can be pure.
It cancels out the sin of hesitation,
restores the flutist's sonorous sensation.

At the Center
MOLLY SIZER

It takes a hot
cup of coffee
and a couple
      of old men

to get me out
of bed mornings
in mid-winter
      at my age.

I brush my teeth
and hair, flash a
grin at my worn
      reflection,

spray a whiff of
scent, and pick a
t-shirt not yet
      grease-splattered.

They're always
early, table
set, tiles face down
      and shaken.

Joe calls me *grrr-*
lie-girl. He can't
remember his
      own mother's

maiden name, but
he recalls downs
from games played five
      weeks ago.

He slams his tiles,
gloats when he scores—
That's a nickel
      girlie-girl

Pete claims status
as my teacher
but still he calls
  me *Missus*—

Don't you mind Joe
he warns. *Not all*
money becomes
  good money.

It's a gloomy
game, with names like
cutthroat, draws from
  a bone yard,

and dominos
in play looking
like one-legged
  skeletons.

Still, it keeps my
brain cells working
and gets me up
  for the day.

The Chairs

REILLY SMITH

Like him, Paw-Paw's chair was an institution;
a navy blue lazy boy—his dutiful second wife.

When he reclined, the springs nagged and the base shrieked.
That chair didn't die; it retired just after him.

His next chair was handed down from Grammy's younger sister;
it held his 3X butt with ease and absorbed the too-loud TV.

That chair ate two hearing aids and eight batteries.
After his hip replacement, the family invested in the last hurrah:

a hospital-grade throne, remote included.
Even with renal failure, he ruined that chair.

Sometimes, when you shift it just right, you can smell
the ammonia-scented humiliation of a man's last stand.

Reading Myself

BRADLEY R. STRAHAN

I am not the man that wrote
those poems praising silken thighs,
all those blue eyes that loved me;
not the whisperer to trees,
glad gardener whose hands
loved the richness of earth.

I've come to that low place on the road
where everything turns against itself:
the ink blotch arms,
the cold shiver hands,
eyes that cannot blink away
the tears of missing names.

I am a skin of bones,
a head of haplessness.
Nothing you ever read
prepares you for this.

Sixty Seconds of Infinity

SANDI STROMBERG

> *The Infinity Room by Yayoi Kusama*
> *—Museum of Fine Arts Houston*

"It's just for one minute," says the museum guard,
opening a door as substantial as those that secure

MRIs and CT scanners. The question of radiation leaps
to mind. "Stand on the triangle," he orders,

assuring this room is only sealed to enhance
Infinity. Out of the dark, hundreds, maybe thousands,

of golden lights fly toward me, tiny lanterns
ceiling to floor. I swivel 360 degrees

as my body shoots through this glorious cosmos
even though my mind knows I'm standing still.

Without warning, the room goes black. I am lost
in space, amorphous, with nothing to measure

myself against. As though gravity had stayed on the other
side of the door. If, as some faiths claim, my body

will transform into energy when I die, will I float
in the vastness of this Universe?

Before I can absorb the possibility,
lanterns burst back into light. My imagination

reels. How can I understand such an unknown
dimension, nowhere to brace or balance?

An unexpected knock. The door opens. I jet back
into *here*, step from the room, blinded for a moment

by Earth's daylight. Vanished, the flash
of immortality. A possible afterlife

I'm not yet ready for.

The Wish
RICK SWANN

At twenty, I wrote that the clear October air
was dry as a wishbone waiting to be snapped.

Now, I wonder at the sadness I felt that autumn
when I discarded days as if they were part

of an endless deck of cards to choose from.
Maybe it was the way blood-red maple leaves

pooled on the ground or knowing that soon
moonlight would slip through bare branches

and cast blue-black shadows on pale snow,
shadows like the veins on the backs of my father's

hands as he lay dying. Now veins spider my hands,
my vision dulls and my hearing fades.

When my own breastbone was split apart
I didn't get to make a wish. If I had, I would

have wished for this—to stand once more
amidst a forest of turning leaves.

Blueberry Picker
LARRY D. THOMAS

Since her husband had died
she'd lived alone in a little cottage.
Each spring, she'd picked her share
of berries with the best of them.

She hated nursing homes, blasting
them as the Grim Reaper's playhouses.
In her ninetieth year, they'd had
a bumper crop of berries big as marbles.

By the time they found her
cushioned by an inch of spilled berries,
she'd already hopscotched the first leg
of her latest, sweet blue journey.

Telemetry
DAVID THOREEN

Asleep, reclining in his hospital bed, my father writes urgently in air—
as if on deadline, though his hand is empty and the sun streaming in.
Two or three thousand, he says evenly, from sleep. Another world there.
Asleep, reclining in his hospital bed, my father writes urgently in air—
ten years he's been retired. I whisper, *I'm here*, run a hand through his hair.
Edema. They've ruled out CHF. They've taken him off the Klonopin.
Asleep, reclining in his hospital bed, my father writes urgently in air—
on deadline, hand empty, sun streaming in.

Aging Interrupted

ULIANA TRYLOWSKY

Is it still considered aging—
If the aging suddenly stops?
If not of illness, but of accident?
If it could have been avoided?

Your hair was gray and thinning,
But your wit was quick.
How could we have known?
You were taken in a turn.

If only he had let me drive.
If only my eyes weren't on the clouds.
If only past were present.
Would your aging have continued?

Where the Time Goes
PAT VALDATA

is down the pile of bricks
and smashed concrete
where we used to sit
and fidget during class:
History is so boring,
we'd complain,
too young to realize
that history was why
our parents' parents came
here in the first place,
because some rich man
in some palace decided
to start a war, starve
the peasants, ogle
their daughters—so
our grandmas and
grandpas packed it in,
sold all they could
for steamship passage
that brought them, finally,
to this town, where as
teenagers we fret about
not having a prom date
or whether that awful
hairstyle will grow out
in time for the class photo,
and not one of us
notices the vultures
circling overhead.

Penultimate Hospital Visit
CLAIRE WEINER

Pastel nothingness. Shifting fluorescence.
Antiseptic sharpness & an engineered drip, drip, drip.

I'd spent years going in and out of rooms like these.
I wasn't put off.

My mother was propped on pillows
like the Victorian heroine she never was. Her left hand—cool,

desiccated, translucent. Her right hand punctured, bruised.
She squeezed my fingers, whispered, "You're here."

A nurse zipped in, busied herself adjusted this,
measured that. "You must be the daughter," she said vaguely.

I looked at my mother, white as milk,
answers to the Friday Times crossword

behind her closed eyes, remembered
the way people used to say we looked alike.

Are We Any Older

LYNN WHITE

Am I any older
my dear, tell me
I cannot tell
can you
tell me,
are you any older,
my dear tell me
if you can
tell,
can you tell?

Can you tell
if we have aged
from the inside out
or the outside in
or is it just on the outside
only on the outside?
I think
we should keep it outside.
Tell me
that we can keep it outside
my dear, tell me.

Skimming the Surface

SCOTT WIGGERMAN

based on Mark Rothko's "Untitled (Blue Divided by Blue)"

Thin white lines curl toward shore across blues without the consistency of rhythm. A lake of intermittent memories. He sounds lucid enough when I call, just sad, as I imagine anyone who's lost a spouse would. Who is ever prepared, especially after sixty-five years of marriage? Waves lift up, tilt down, undercurrents from nine decades of existence. Deep waters to draw from in this selective lake where bad memories have sunk, at rest in the unreachable mud and muck.

Over the months, he repeats several times how he and my mother never once fought. I know better, recall covering my ears with my palms in a dark closet as they screamed at each other. Better calm waves than crashing ones, better lonely than angry, so I don't contradict him. Let him believe what he wants. He repeats stories, tiresome as waves. In truth, I've had more conversations with my father than I ever had before my mother's passing.

Until my sister's call, I never deemed anything amiss. Suddenly I hear about maggots overtaking his kitchen, foreclosure notices, unpaid utilities, unwashed dishes, soiled clothing. Waves of disconnect between the lonely man I talk with on the phone and the one my brothers and sister experience. Crashing waves, the white gap widens.

pull
       of the undertow
                    further offshore

Pages from a Wall Calendar

JOHN WILLSON

> *"Snail, snail, glister me forward..."*
> *—Theodore Roethke, The Lost Son*

November is a snail on bamboo.
Between two of the stem's held breaths,
the ridge on the joint has diverted the snail's
upward progress. The shell blazes, a spiral
yellow on green.

December is a stone that stands
among other stones, white gravel
raked in ripples around them. Stones
and white gravel, the Zen garden fills the pool
where the greenhouse poet died swimming.

Snow-slick roads of January having kept
me two weeks from swimming, I enter the pool
slowly, stretch my arms backward, minding
the rotator cuff. A year older
than my father when pneumonia

and a coronary took him, I push off, goggles
trained on the black line, the first lap underwater.
How would it feel, water flowing into these lungs?
I near the cross-mark at the deep end, rise,
coil, burst out of the turn.

A Cascading, it is

STEVE WILSON

to watch his memory falter,

      fail. Light fades and falls. Dark

to watch his memory falter—

        Cans of beans: gone. Toothpaste.

        A shoe, bills, a sister—

to watch his memory falter,

      fail. Light fades, and falls dark.

Old Man Preps for Road Trip

JERRY WINAKUR

Once more it's summer and time—
after 3 years chopped off my shrinking life—
to take a trip somewhere
not necessarily grand but wherever
and—like summers of old—we'll need a cooler.

I know just where it is out in the garage
the blue plastic one we used on those
weekend fishing trips down to the coast
when the kids were small
the one we put the fish in as soon as
they came flopping out of the bay
right before they were filleted.

But when I pull the thing
off the shelf the handle
breaks off in my grasp
and the drain plug
crumbles like chalk in my hand
like the osteoporotic bones of my spine
that diminish me year by year.

Why I stood there for a moment
staring at the devastation
time has wrought I don't know
except maybe to delay the inevitable trip
to Wal-Mart but I finally go
only to find the same cheap shit coolers
like the one I just put out to the curb

plastic hinges and pop rivets
not a piece of metal to be found
and okay I don't think I've got
all that many summers left in me...
But still.

The next aisle over displays the Deeluxe models—
named after Sasquatch who himself wouldn't be
caught dead hauling around one of these tarted up things...
Can you believe two hundred and fifty bucks for
a freakin' cooler—and still plastic and rubber
and bullshit is what this world is comin' to...
I just couldn't plunk down the moola.
Driving home I'm scratching my head

while a memory struggles out of a sinkhole:
those summers long ago before the house the kids
before we needed vacations
when all we had was a blue
VW bug jammed with a 2-man surplus army pup tent
a gasoline stove a couple of cotton sleeping bags
metal canteens...and wasn't there a cooler?

I know everything is long gone—the detritus of a past life
but I'm thinking: attic, attic
though I haven't been
up there in decades afraid of being unable to get down
but what the hell
and damn if I'm spending 250 bucks
on a piece of shit cooler.

And I don't give a rat's ass
if I die up there 'cause I damn well know
there are worse places to die.
So I carry the ladder through the house and up three flights
of stairs—thankfully you're out for the day
or I'd be tongue-lashed—
and for the record: YES I am a stupid old fart should you find
me splayed out somewhere.

The attic door springs up after only a minor head butt
not quite enough to cause a brain bleed
and I haul my dually-assed self up inside and flail
my arm around searching for the string to pull
so the light will come on
but of course it doesn't
and with the third yank the strand breaks
away from the fixture and that should be that
since my executive function has declined to the point where
I didn't stick a flashlight in my back pocket before all this...

But just then—
and you won't believe it since I sure as hell didn't—
the sun reaches some perfect angle and light pours into the attic through
the roof vent throwing a bright beam back into the corner
where it falls where it illumines like in a medieval painting
not the Child or his Mother but a goddamn fire engine red
steel Coleman cooler with stainless handles
and hinges and even built-in bottle-openers on both sides!
God, it reminds me of that 1960 Corvette Stingray

those boys drove on Route 66. The one I coveted
but never ever got. Nothing even close unless you count
the used orange Suburban I rattled around in for fifteen years.

Okay it's dusty
and there are a few barnacles on it that look a lot
like the things the dermatologist burns off my arms
every year and the handles squeak
and the lining is yellowed here and there like my teeth.
But it'll clean up real nice—
a little detergent, bleach, WD 40, elbow grease
and the thing will last us forever or at least until
I'm in a cooler of my own.

Final note to wife:
just freakin' bury me in this one
when the time comes.
The way things are going
by then I'll for sure fit.

Dance of Oaks

CLARENCE WOLFSHOHL

Saturday nights the old folks scrub the dirt
from under their nails, as best they can,
wear dress comfortable shoes, go dance,
go to St. Hedwig or Liederkranz Hall,
go to talk crops and rain, go to drink beer—
beer barreled belly farmers and their wives
in clean starched cotton dresses like lampshades
glowing on the dance floor for this night.

Some people dance like saplings in the morning breezes,
sliding between other couples softly,
silent their steps in the hush of the dance,
and the music slips through them like their hands.

These farmers are oaks in the morning breeze,
grand in their resistance, creaking their limbs
knotted with fibers hard to the core,
the polka pumping to the beat of their hearts.

The old folks hop slower than the band,
heaving movements like tree crowns
lifted a gust of wind at a time, a half-beat behind
the wind's song. They have grown thick, grown deep,
oaks dancing the polka.

CONTRIBUTORS

ROBERT ALLEN studied creative writing at the University of Texas at Austin. His poems have appeared in *Lone Star Poetry, Voices de la Luna, Texas Poetry Assignment, Texas Poetry Calendar, di-vêrsé-city, The Ocotillo Review,* and *the San Antonio Express-News.* Three times he has been featured in VIA's Poetry on the Move contest. He is retired and lives with his family in San Antonio, where once each month he facilitates Gemini Ink's in-person Open Writer's Lab. His poem "Possibilities" is original to this publication.

LINDA ANGELO came late to the writing of poetry, having spent her growing up years in quiet introspection, her professional years practicing psychotherapy, and her creative energies channeled into painting. Her poem "Coda" is original to this publication.

SHELLEY ARMITAGE, emerita professor, is the author of eight award-winning books, the most recent *Walking the Llano: A Texas Memoir of Place and A Habit of Landscape.* She held the Distinguished Chair in American Literature Fulbright in Warsaw, Fulbright awards in Finland and Portugal, National Endowment for the Humanities and National Endowment for the Arts grants, and a Rockefeller grant. She manages the family grasslands near Vega, Texas. Her poem "I'm As Old As Turtles" is original to this publication.

CARL AUERBACH is an emeritus Professor of Psychology at Yeshiva University, specializing in the psychology of trauma, with an emphasis on collective trauma and mass violence. His poetry has been published in many literary journals. His poem "On Having a Body" is original to this publication.

ALEX BARR's recent poetry is in *Last Stanza Poetry Journal, Quagmire Magazine, Poetry Review, The MacGuffin, Scintilla, The Dark Horse, Orbis, Silver Birch Press, BlueHouse Journal, Hole in the Head Review, Acumen,* and *Ground Journal.* His poetry collections are *Letting in the Carnival* from Peterloo, *Henry's Bridge* from Starborn, and *Bedding Plants For My Father* from Cerasus. He is co-author of *Orchards,* a verse translation of Rilke's French poetry sequence *Vergers* published by Starborn. He lives in Wales. His poem "Graphology" is original to this publication.

ALAN BERECKA is a retired librarian who currently lives in Sinton, Texas. His poems have appeared in journals such as the *Red River Review, Ruminate, The Christian Century,* and *Texas Review.* He has published six books of poetry, the latest is *Atlas Sighs: Selected and New Poems*, Turning Plow Press, 2024. His poem "The Flip Side" is original to this publication.

JERRY BRADLEY is a retired professor of English. A member of the Texas Institute of Letters, he is the author of ten books including most recently *Rapunzel's Parrot*. His poems have appeared in *New England Review, Modern Poetry Studies*, and *Southern Humanities Review*. He was the long-time poetry editor of *Concho River Review*. He now lives in Bluffton, South Carolina. His poem "Doctors" is original to this publication.

After retiring from teaching English at San Jose State University, SHARON V. BROWN moved to the beautiful Pacific Northwest, where she has returned to her passion for writing poetry. She recently joined the Greenwood Poets Group in Seattle, Washington, and has begun honing her craft with the enriched perspective of an older woman. Her poem "An Old Man Sleeps" is original to this publication.

A former journalist, CAROL FLAKE CHAPMAN returned to poetry, her first love, after the sudden death of her husband on a wild river in Guatemala shattered her life. Poetry, she found, was the language she needed not only for her healing but to respond to a world gone haywire. She has published three books of poetry, and her poems have been included in numerous journals and anthologies, including a medical journal. Her poem "Silver Alert" is original to this publication.

BARBARA CHILCOTE lives in Seattle where she writes about coffee, her friends, and gardening. She recently fell on a sidewalk in Paris and broke her writing shoulder. Like all of us, she carries on. Her poem "In Sickness" is original to this publication.

PETER CHRISTENSEN has published six books of poetry—*Hailstorm, Rig Talk, To Die Ascending, Oona River Poems*, and *The Circle of Willis*—as well as a bestseller book of short stories, *Wilderness Tales*. He was a Writer in Residence at Banff Centre, Okanagan University College, and Wallace Stegner House. A new poetry collection *Birds of Prey* has just been completed and is looking for a publisher. His poem "Hunger" is original to this publication.

BARBARA CROOKER is the author of twelve chapbooks and ten full-length books of poetry, including *Some Glad Morning*, Pitt Poetry Series, University of Pittsburgh Poetry Press, longlisted for the Julie Suk award from Jacar Press, *The Book of Kells*, which won the Best Poetry Book of 2019 Award from Poetry by the Sea, and *Slow Wreckage*, forthcoming from Grayson Books. Her other awards include: Grammy Spoken Word Finalist, the WB Yeats Society of New York Award, the Thomas Merton Poetry of the Sacred Award, and three Pennsylvania Council fellowships in literature. Her work appears in literary journals and anthologies, including *The Bedford Introduction to Literature*. Her poem "Weight Training" originally appeared in *Verse-Virtual*.

SHARON CUMBERLAND is a poet and Emeritus Professor of English at Seattle University where she taught literature and directed the creative writing program. She has published widely and written three collections of poems including the recent *Found In A Letter 1959* from Ex Ophidia Press, 2022. Her poem "On My 75th Birthday" is original to this publication.

JANELLE CURLIN-TAYLOR is a native Texan, actress, mycologist, therapist, pastoral counselor, minister, and poet. Her poems have been published in *di-verse-city Anthology, Blue Hole Anthology, Best Austin Poetry 2018-2019, Waco Wordfest Anthology, Texas Poetry Calendar, Voices de la Luna, Lone Star Poetry Anthology, Tejascovido*, and *Texas Poetry Assignment*. Her poem "Old Habits" is original to this publication.

CHIP DAMERON is the author of eleven collections of poetry and a travel journal. His poems, as well as his essays on contemporary writers, have appeared in numerous publications in the U.S. and abroad. His most recent book is *Relatively Speaking: Poems of Person and Place*, which combines a collection of his poems with a collection by poet Betsy Joseph. A member of the Texas Institute of Letters, he also was a writer in residence for four months at the Dobie Paisano ranch. He is a professor emeritus of English at UT Rio Grande Valley and lives in Georgetown. His poem "For Gene, Gone at 82" is original to this publication.

LORNE DANIEL lives in Victoria, British Columbia. He has published four books of poetry, edited anthologies, and served as Writer in Residence at the University of Lethbridge. His poem "Crushed" was a featured Poetry Month 'postcard poem' (distributed by the League of Canadian Poets) in 2019. His poem "Biking to the Green Burial Grounds" was originally published in *Juniper*.

MARGO DAVIS explores the arts and other countries. Her poems have appeared in *The Ekphrastic Review, Deep South Magazine*,

Midwest Quarterly, Panoply, Fourth River, MockingHeart Review, and *Odes and Elegies: Eco-Poetry from the Texas Gulf Coast.* Her chapbook is entitled *Quicksilver.* Margo lives in Houston. Her poem "Bedside Vigil" is original to this publication.

YSABEL DE LA ROSA is a writer and poet whose work has appeared in numerous publications. anthologies, and websites, including *Calyx, Nimrod, Poem, Anderbo, Wisconsin Review, Panoply,* and *Phoebe,* and the anthologies, *Houston Poetry Fest, Texas Weather, Her Texas,* and *Texas Poetry Calendar.* Her poem "Safe House" was awarded Best Poem by the Press Women of Texas and the National Federation of Press Women in 2022. Her poem "What Now Then" is original to this publication.

GERALDINE DELUCA is a retired teacher and writer. She has published *Teaching Toward Freedom: Voices and Silence in the English Classroom,* many academic essays and interviews, and co-founded and edited a journal about children's literature, *The Lion and the Unicorn: a Critical Journal of Children's Literature.* She has also published short stories and poems. Her poem "The Yard Sale" is original to this publication.

STANLEY E. DENNY is a resident of San Angelo, Texas, and is a graduate of the University of Texas at Austin where he received a BA in Liberal Arts. He has been published by *Voices de la Luna, Better Than Starbucks, Cattails,* and *The Cherita.* His poem "Gerontion" is original to this publication.

WINSTON DERDEN is a poet and fiction writer residing in Houston, Texas. His poetry has been published in *Barbaric Yawp, SoftCartel, Plum Tree Tavern, Backchannels, Pure Slush, New Reader Magazine, MONO, Book of Matches, Molecule,* and numerous anthologies. He holds a BA and MA from the University of Texas, Austin. His poem "Whispering to Mnemosyne" is original to this publication.

JESSE DOIRON has worked in America, Europe, the Middle East, and Eurasia as an educator and consultant. His teaching experience ranges from English for international business at UC-Berkeley Extension in San Francisco to creative writing at Mark Stiles Maximum Security Prison for the Texas Department of Criminal Justice. His poem "Damned Spring" was originally published in *Texas Poetry Assignment.*

JUDITH R. DUNCAN retired from software development ten years ago while living in Chicago, IL. She is pleased to live in the snowy woods of the Olympic Peninsula, WA., and to have just celebrated her 79th birthday. Judith lives on five wooded acres with her spouse and pets. Her major activity is tending a fruit orchard, hiking, writing poems, and reading. Her poem "When I Was Young" is original to this publication.

WENDY DUNMEYER's full-length collection, *My Grandmother's Last Letter*, is from Lamar University Literary Press. Her work also has appeared in *Measure, Natural Bridge, The Oklahoma Review, Cumberland River Review*, and elsewhere. She nurtures emerging writers in many ways, including volunteering as a visiting writer for National Poetry Month at local elementary schools and encouraging undergraduate student writers from Cameron University, Lawton, Oklahoma. The poem "Elderly Woman Rocking" is from her book *My Grandmother's Last Letter*.

LISKEN VAN PELT DUS teaches languages, writing, and martial arts in western Massachusetts. Her poetry can be found in many journals, including recently *Third Wednesday Magazine, Sky Island Journal, The Comstock Review, Eunoia Review, Amethyst Review*, and the *1455's Movable Type*; and in anthologies such as the *Crafty Poet Anthology Series*. Recent translations can also be found in *Epiphany*. Books include *What We're Made Of* (Cherry Grove, 2016) and a chapbook, *Letters to My Dead* (Three Bunny Farms, 2022). The poem "Frost" is from *Letters to My Dead*.

CHRIS ELLERY is the author of six poetry collections, most recently *One Like Silence, Elder Tree,* and *Canticles of the Body*. A member of the Texas Institute of Letters, he has received the X.J. Kennedy Award for Nonfiction, the Dora and Alexander Raynes Prize, the Betsy Colquitt Award, and the Texas Poetry Prize. His poem "Daughter Heaven Mountain" is from *One Like Silence*.

KELLY ANN ELLIS holds an MA in English Literature from the University of Houston, where she also taught for over a decade. Her poetry, which has appeared in numerous journals and anthologies, was featured in the REELpoetry festival for three consecutive years and showcased at the Houston Fringe Festival in 2019. Her poetry collection, *The Hungry Ghost Diner*, was published by Lamar University Literary Press in 2023. Her poem "Burnt Dust" is from *The Hungry Ghost Diner*.

MAUREEN TOLMAN FLANNERY splits her time between Chicago and Wyoming where she and her husband Dan have rescued and restored three historic log cabins. Her latest poetry collection is *Already Part of the Sky*, about her ranch upbringing and the history of the cattle war in Johnson County. Her poetry also appears in *North American Review, Xavier Review, Winning Writers, BorderSenses, Wisconsin Review, Birmingham Poetry Review, Santa Fe Literary Review, Calyx, Pedestal*, and *Atlanta Review*. Her poem "Time After Time" is original to this publication.

ELIZABETH N. FLORES, Professor Emeritus of Political Science, taught for over 40 years at Del Mar College and was the college's first Mexican American Studies Program Coordinator. Her poems have appeared in the *Texas Poetry Assignment, Corpus Christi Writers* (2022 and 2023 editions) anthologies edited by William Mays, *the Mays Publishing Literary Magazine*, and *Windward Review*. Her poem "Questions" is original to this publication.

DEDE FOX's writing credits include *The Woodlands Art Benches*, a coffee table book from Typing Monkey Publishers, 2023. Lamar University Literary Press published *On Wings of Silence: Mexico '68*, a novel in verse, in 2019. TCU Press published her first novel *The Treasure in the Tiny Blue Tin*. Other works include poetry in *Postcards Home, Confessions of a Jewish Texan*, and nonfiction in *Highlights*. Her poem "Birthday" is original to this publication.

CYNTHIA READ GARDNER attended Greens Farms Academy and holds degrees from Simon's Rock College (AA), Simmons College (BA), and Smith College School for Social Work (MSW). She has been employed as a clinical social worker since 1975. She has a private practice and has worked as a Clinical Juvenile Court Clinician in Pittsfield, MA for the past 26 years. She was married for 38 years, was recently widowed, and has two adult sons. Her poem "Luella" is original to this publication.

ELISA A. GARZA is a poet and editor from Houston with family roots in South Texas. Her full-length collection, *Regalos*, is forthcoming from Lamar University Literary Press and was a finalist for the National Poetry Series. Her most recent chapbook, *Between the Light / entre la claridad*, is in a second edition from Mouthfeel Press. Elisa has been awarded a Literature Fellowship from the Texas Commission on the Arts and the Emerging Writer Award from the Alfredo Cisneros del Moral Foundation. She taught writing and literature for many years to students from elementary through senior citizens. Her poem "Microcosm" is original to this publication.

MATTHEW GRAHAM is the author of four books of poetry, most recently *The Geography of Home* from the Galileo Press. He served as the Indiana State Poet Laureate from 2020 through 2023. His poem "Wonderful Life" is original to this publication.

AMY L. GREENSPAN spent much of her career writing and editing law books. Her poems appear in multiple editions of the *Texas Poetry Calendar* and in collections including *Waco Wordfest Anthology 2023, Texas Poetry Assignment, Weaving the Terrain: 100-Word Southwestern Poems, Lifting the Sky: Southwestern Haiku and Haiga, cattails,* and *Haiku Presence.* Her poem "Prayer for My Aging Senses" is original to this publication.

JEAN HACKETT lives and writes in San Antonio and the Texas Hill Country. Her most recent work has appeared in journals *Plants and Poetry* and *Voices de la Luna*, anthologies *The Stars and Moon in the Evening Sky, Purifying Wind, No Season for Silence, Easing the Edges,* and *Yellow Flag*, as well as *Arts Alive San Antonio*. Her chapbook *Masked/Unmuted* was published in March 2022. Her poem "Widow's Words Unspoken" is original to this publication.

SISTER LOU ELLA HICKMAN's poems have appeared in *America, US Catholic, Commonweal, The Christian Century, Prism,* and several anthologies. Press 53 published her first book of poetry entitled *she: robed and wordless* in 2015. Five of the poems were set to music and performed at 92Y in New York City on May 11, 2021, and a second concert was held in Cleveland, Ohio on March 28, 2023. Her poem "the painting woman and child on a balcony" is original to this publication.

VINCENT HOSTAK is a poet, essayist, and media producer. He's held long-time residences in Austin and Colorado, where he's also worked in documentary and network television/film production. His poetry may be found in the print journals *Sonder Midwest (#5)/Illinois, The Langdon Review of the Arts in Texas*, and the 2022/2023 anthology *Lone Star Poetry: Championing Texas Verse, Community and Hunger Relief.* He is currently appointed to the 2024 editorial team at *Asymptote*, an international journal dedicated to the art of English language translations of contemporary world literature. He's a two-time Summer Scholar at Naropa University's Summer Writing Program, directed by Anne Waldman. His poem "Recollection" is original to this publication.

JARED HOUZE is a seventh-generation Texan who grew up in Dallas and currently lives in Amarillo with his wife and three children. His poems and other writings have appeared in *Earth & Altar Magazine* and *Spirit of Abilene*. His poem "Shaving with the Ancestors" is original to this publication.

CAROLYN HOWE has been writing poetry and painting in watercolor since her retirement as a sociology professor at the College of the Holy Cross. She has published a chapbook, *Across the Street*. She is a member of the Rosemont Street Poetry Workshop and the Worcester County Poetry Association. Her poem "Aging Painter" originally appeared in *Across the Street*.

SABA HUSAIN is a Pakistani-American poet. She is the author of *Elegy for My Tongue* (Terrapin Books, 2023). Her work appears in numerous literary journals. Saba was the 2022 Spring Equinox Hot Poet's Poetry Competition winner and received the 2020 Editor's Choice Award from Lamar University Press. Saba works a day job and is a board member of Mutabilis Press. She holds a B.A. in Creative Writing from the University of Houston. Her poem "The Bird in the Pesunia Tree, and the Clock" is original to this publication.

KATHRYN JONES is a poet, journalist, and essayist whose work has been published in *The New York Times, Texas Monthly,* and many other publications. Her poetry has appeared in literary journals and anthologies, including TexasPoetryAssignment.org, *Unknotting the Line: The Poetry in Prose* (Dos Gatos Press, 2023), and *Lone Star Poetry* (Kallisto Gaia Press, 2023). A chapbook, *An Orchid's Guide to Life*, is forthcoming from Finishing Line Press in August 2024. Jones was inducted into the Texas Institute of Letters and lives on a ranch near Glen Rose, Texas. Her poem "That Night in the Davis Mountains" originally appeared in *Texas Poetry Assignment*.

LIBBY FALK JONES's recent poetry books include *For Your Good Health, Drink Flowers* (Bass Clef Books, 2023), and *Yakety Yak (Don't Talk Back)* (Workhorse, 2022). Her poems and creative nonfiction have been published in more than 25 journals and anthologies. A professor emerita of English at Berea College and past president of the Kentucky State Poetry Society, she lives and writes in Berea, KY, where she co-directs a writing project for Kentucky women over 60. Her poem "Local Warming" is original to this publication.

MILTON JORDAN lives with Anne in a Senior Living facility in Georgetown, Texas. He has published poems in chapbooks, collections, and journals for over 50 years. His poem "Relearning the Language" first appeared in The Wesleyan.

BETSY JOSEPH lives in Dallas and has poems that have appeared in a number of journals and anthologies. She is the author of two poetry books published by Lamar University Literary Press: *Only So Many Autumns* (2019) and most recently, *Relatively Speaking* (2022), a collaborative collection with her brother, poet Chip Dameron. Her poem "Palimpsests" first appeared in *Texas Poetry Assignment*.

CAROL KANTER's poetry has appeared in over seventy literary journals and anthologies. Finishing Line Press published her first two chapbooks, *Out of Southern Africa* and *Chronicle of Dog*. Peterborough Poetry Project published her third, *Of Water*. Her poem "Waiting for MRIs" is original to this publication.

IRENE KELLER has taught writing and literature to secondary and community college students in Texas public schools, and she enjoyed helping students gain confidence in their writing abilities. Retired, she now has time to write poetry, often about experiences and people in hopes they are not forgotten. Her poem "Connections with Life in Spite of Dementia" is original to this publication.

TINA KELLEY's *Rise Wildly* appeared in 2020 from CavanKerry Press, joining *Abloom & Awry, Precise*, and *The Gospel of Galore*, a Washington State Book Award winner. She reported for *The New York Times* and wrote two nonfiction books. Her poems have appeared in *Cimarron Review, Southwest Review, Prairie Schooner*, and *The Best American Poetry 2009*, among other publications. She received a 2023 Finalist award from the New Jersey State Council on the Arts. Her poem "Don't Die In" is original to this publication.

Farm girl, rock climber, and professor, KAREN KILCUP feels fortunate to be getting old. Her book *The Art of Restoration* (2023) was awarded the 2021 Winter Goose Poetry Prize, and her chapbook, *Red Appetite* (2023), received the 2022 Helen Kay Poetry Chapbook Prize. She has recently published a second chapbook, *Black Nebula*, and has a forthcoming collection, *Feathers and Wedges*. Her poem "Old Ice" is original to this publication.

KATE KINGSTON is the author of five collections of poetry. Her most recent book, *The Future Wears Camouflage*, is forthcoming from Salmon Poetry in 2024. She is the recipient of the Karen Chamberlain Award, the W.D. Snodgrass Award for Poetic Endeavor and

Excellence, the Ruth Stone Prize, and the Atlanta Review International Publication Prize. Kingston has been awarded fellowships from the Colorado Council on the Arts, Harwood Museum, Helene Wurlitzer Foundation, Jentel, Ucross, and Fundación Valparaíso in Mojácar, Spain, among others. Her poem "Metaphors in Disaster" is original to this publication.

CRAIG KINNEY was born and raised in suburbia in Houston, Texas, and lived in Austin and New York, but thankfully moved to West Texas in 1997, where he tries to age gracefully with his wife Susan and their two dogs. An architect by trade, he currently works on smaller-scale projects such as houses and renovations. As these years pass, Craig is thrilled to be able to spend more time reading, writing, drawing, swimming, and hanging out. His poem "The Mattress" is original to this publication.

LAURIE KOLP is an educator, avid reader, runner, and nature lover living in Southeast Texas. She is the author of *Upon the Blue Couch* and *Hello, It's Your Mother*. Her poems have appeared in *Whale Road Review, SWWIM, The Inflectionist Review*, and more. Her poem "Wordless" is original to this publication.

JIM LAVILLA-HAVELIN is the author of six books of poetry, the most recent: *Tales from the Breakaway Republic* (Moonstone Press, 2022). LaVilla-Havelin is a community arts activist, editor, and educator. He teaches senior citizens and incarcerated youth. He is the Coordinator for National Poetry Month in San Antonio. His poem "After All" is original to this publication.

MARY MAKOFSKE's latest books are *No Angels* (Kelsay, 2023), *The Gambler's Daughter* (The Orchard Street Press, 2022); *World Enough, and Time* (Kelsay, 2017); and *Traction* (Ashland, 2011), winner of the Richard Snyder Prize. Her poems have appeared in more than 70 journals including *Poetry, Poetry East, American Journal of Poetry, Southern Poetry Review, Comstock Review, Mississippi Review, Louisville Review, Valparaiso Poetry Review*, and in 21 anthologies. Her poem "Sweet, Bitter, Bittersweet" first appeared in *World Enough, and Time*.

LYNN MARTIN's work has appeared in *The Antioch Review, Poetry Northwest, Southern Poetry Review, Bitterroot, Indiana Review, Blind Donkey, Hunger Mountain, Chicago Quarterly Review*, and *Chariton Review*. Her prizes include the Ernest L. Parker Medallion of Merit and the Spence Poetry Prize. She studied Dante in Italy after winning a National Endowment for the Humanities Fellowship. Her poetry collections are, *Where the Yellow Field Widened: Elegies for a Lost Child*, and *Blue Bowl*. She lives in Gig Harbor, Washington. Her poem "Elemental Elegy" is original to this publication.

DON MATHIS' life revolves around the many poetry circles in San Antonio. His poems have been published in many anthologies and periodicals and broadcast on local television and national radio. He has also written policies and procedures for industrial clients, case histories for psychological firms, and news and reviews for various media. His poem "Shades of Grey" is original to this publication.

JEAN A. MCARTHUR lives in Austin, Texas, and works as a computer programmer at the University of Texas. Her avocations have included whitewater kayaking and playing in international Scrabble tournaments, and many of her poems are stories about kayak trips and tournaments. Three years ago she started writing a poem a week, and they're usually inspired by dredged up from memories of people and incidents. Her poem "I Never Saw Her Dance" is original to this publication.

JANET MCCANN is a crone poet who taught at Texas A&M University for 47 years. Her latest poetry book is *Life List* (Wipf and Stock, 2020). Her poem "The Ghosts" is original to this publication.

A Pushcart honoree, with a personal essay in Pushcart Prize XLII, DAVID MEISCHEN is the author of *Nopalito: Stories* (University of New Mexico Press 2024) and *Caliche Road Poems* (Lamar University Literary Press 2024). *Anyone's Son* (3: A Taos Press 2020) won Best First Book of Poetry from the Texas Institute of Letters. A former juror for the Kimmel Harding Nelson Center for the Arts, David has had a writing residency at Jentel Arts. Co-founder and Managing Editor of Dos Gatos Press, he lives in Albuquerque, NM with his husband—also his co-publisher and co-editor—Scott Wiggerman. His poem "A Glance in Her Direction" is original to this publication.

MoonPath Press published KEVIN MILLER's *Spring Meditation* in 2022. Miller's *Vanish* won the Wandering Aengus Press Publication Award in 2019. He lives in Tacoma, WA. His poem "This is Me" is original to this publication.

TERRY JUDE MILLER received the 2018 Catherine Case Lubbe Manuscript Prize for his book, *The Drawn Cat's Dream*. His work has been published in the *Southern Poetry Anthology, The Lily Poetry*

Review, The Comstock Review, and *The Oakland Review* and in scores of other publications. He serves as 1st Vice Chancellor for the National Federation of State Poetry Societies. His poem "Song of Joy" is original to this publication.

LOUISE MOISES is an award-winning poet, who has been published in literary journals and anthologies including *California Quarterly, Tiny Seed,* and *High Shelf Press*. She began writing poetry as a means of grieving, having been widowed for a second time. She has since explored other themes and is especially inspired by travels in her motor home. Her poem "Peace Is" was the grand prize winner in *Artist Embassy International Dancing Poetry*. Her first chapbook will be published in Spring 2024 by Finishing Line Press. Her poem "Morning Dance" is original to this publication.

JOHN MORGAN studied with Robert Lowell at Harvard, where he won the Hatch Prize for Lyric Poetry. At the Iowa Writers' Workshop, he earned his M.F.A. and was awarded the Academy of American Poets Prize. In 1976, he moved to Fairbanks, Alaska, to direct the creative writing program at the University of Alaska. He has published eight collections of poetry and his work has appeared in *The New Yorker, Poetry, The American Poetry Review, The New Republic, The Paris Review*, and many other journals. He and his wife Nancy now divide their time between Fairbanks and Bellingham, Washington. His poem "Stray Thoughts on Aging" originally appeared in Crab Orchard Review.

SUZANNE MORRIS is a novelist with eight published works, and a poet. Her poems have appeared in anthologies including *Lone Star Poetry* (Kallisto Gaia Press, 2023), and online poetry journals including *The Texas Poetry Assignment, The New Verse News,* and *Stone Poetry Quarterly*. Ms. Morris resides in Cherokee County, Texas. Her poem "Confabulation" is original to this publication.

WILDA MORRIS, Workshop Chair of Poets and Patrons of Chicago and a past President of the Illinois State Poetry Society, has published numerous poems in anthologies, webzines, and print publications, including *Turtle Island Quarterly, Modern Haiku,* and *Journal of Modern Poetry*. She has won awards for formal and free verse and haiku, including the 2019 Founders' Award from the National Federation of State Poetry Societies. She has published three books of poetry: *Szechwan Shrimp and Fortune Cookies: Poems from a Chinese Restaurant* (RWG Press), *Pequod Poems: Gaming with Moby-Dick* (Kelsay Books), and *At Goat Hollow and Other Poems*

(Kelsay). Her poem "On the Trail, Door County, September" is original to this publication.

CAROL LOUISE MUNN lives and writes in Houston, Texas. She earned her MFA in creative writing at the University of Michigan. Her poems have appeared in many journals including *Poetry, The GSU Review, Fugue, WomenArts Quarterly Journal, Poetry Quarterly, Ampersand Review, The Chaffin Journal, 10X3 plus, Lascaux Review, The Texas Poetry Calendar,* and *The Midwest Quarterly Review.* Recently, her poems were published in *Iris Literary Journal, Comstock Review, Equinox – Vol. 5,* and *Slab Literary Magazine* (Slippery Rock University.) Her poem "Mourning at the Kaldi Café" originally appeared in *String Poet Journal.*

JANICE O'MAHONY grew up around the world in a large Air Force family. She majored in Anthropology and Chemistry, then got an MSW to make a living. She spent her career as an advocate for marginalized people and sensible, humane public policy. She now lives on an island on the Salish Sea and writes what she wants. Her poem "Moving Day" is original to this publication.

Irish-Australian poet NATHANAEL O'REILLY teaches creative writing at the University of Texas at Arlington. His twelve collections include *Dublin Wandering* (Recent Work Press, 2024), *Landmarks* (Lamar University Literary Press, 2024), *Selected Poems of Ned Kelly* (Downingfield Press, 2024), *Boulevard* (Downingfield Press, 2024), *(Un)belonging* (Recent Work Press, 2020), and *Preparations for Departure* (UWAP, 2017). His work appears in journals and anthologies published in fifteen countries. He is poetry editor for *Antipodes: A Global Journal of Australian/New Zealand Literature.* His poem "The Body Remembers" originally appeared in *Howl: New Irish Writing.*

Born in Galveston, Texas, MICHAEL OWENS writes from his home in Cypress, Texas. His poem "Service" is original to this publication.

PETER PEREIRA is a poet and family physician in Seattle, Washington. His poems have appeared in *Poetry, Virginia Quarterly Review, Prairie Schooner,* and have been featured on BBC Radio, The Writer's Almanac, and in the *Best American Poetry* anthology. His books include *Saying the World,* and *What's Written on the Body,* both from Copper Canyon Press. His poem "Companion Animals" is original to this publication.

CELESTE PFISTER has long been writing in the shadows of her roles including mother, physician, teacher, mentor, writer, artist, and musician. She has taught literary courses and had essays published in *Reunion* (Shodair Children's Hospital). She publishes a bi-weekly blog, "Creative Inspiration," on topics of art and poetry. She lives in Venice, Florida where she paints, and is working on her first poetry collection and a memoir. Her poem "Vanishing Point" is original to this publication.

D. ELLIS PHELPS' poems, essays, and visual art have appeared widely online and in print. She has taught fine arts to students of all ages for decades & currently facilitates writing craft workshops for local libraries. Author of four poetry collections: *what she holds* (Moon Shadow Sanctuary Press, 2020), *what holds her* (Main Street Rag, 2019), *words gone wild* (Kelsay Books, 2021), and *of failure & faith* (Kelsay Books, 2023), and the novel, *Making Room for George* (MSSP 2016), she is also founding editor of Moon Shadow Sanctuary Press and *fws: international journal of literature & art*. Her poem "slow dissolve" is original to this publication.

SYLVIA BYRNE POLLACK's poems appear in *The Stillwater Review, Crab Creek Review, Wild Roof*, and other journals. She's a 2019 Jack Straw Writer and 2021 Mineral School Resident. Both her debut collection *Risking It* (2021) and her latest book, *What Lasts* (2023) are from Red Mountain Press. Her poem "Holdfast" is from *What Lasts*.

KYLE POTVIN's debut full-length poetry collection is *Loosen* (Hobblebush Books, 2021). Her chapbook, *Sound Travels on Water*, won the Jean Pedrick Chapbook Award. Her poems have appeared in *Bellevue Literary Review, Tar River Poetry, Ecotone*, and *The New York Times*. She is a peer reviewer for *Whale Road Review*. Kyle lives on the seacoast of New Hampshire. Her poem "Memorial of Bone" originally appeared in *THINK*.

DONNA PUCCIANI, a Chicago-based writer, has published poetry worldwide in *Shi Chao Poetry, Poetry Salzburg, Acumen, ParisLitUp, Mediterranean Poetry, Meniscus, Journal of Italian Translation*, and other journals. Her seventh and latest book of poetry is *Edges*. Her poem "The years advance" originally appeared in *Front Range Review*.

ELENA LELIA RADULESCU is a Romanian-American writer. Her poetry, essays and short stories have been published by *Vi-*

sions *International, Square Lake Review, The Spoon River Poetry Review, Chelsea, Karamu, CALYX Journal, Trajectory Journal, The Cape Rock Review, Magnolia Journal, Gastronomica Journal, Third Wednesday Journal, Concho River Review, Ocotillo Journal, Voices de la Luna, Evening Street Journal, The Blue Earth Review, North Dakota Review* and other literary publications. Her poem "His Rubber Boots" is original to this publication.

MINDY REED is a novelist, poet, editor, and radio host of the weekly program: *Writing on the Air.* She is a retired librarian and founder of The Authors' Assistant. Her published works include *Women of a Certain Age: Stories of the 20th Century* and *This is the Dawning: a Woodstock Love Story.* Her poem "Older but not Wiser" is original to this publication.

EVE RIFKAH is co-founder of Poetry Oasis, Inc., a non-profit poetry association dedicated to educating and promoting local poets. Founder, and editor of *Diner*, a literary magazine, she is the 2021 recipient of the Stanley Kunitz Award. She lives in Worcester, MA. The play, *Outcasts the Lepers of Penikese Island*, was based on her first book. Her poem "doing battle" is original to this publication.

DARBY RILEY practices law in San Antonio with his son, Charles. He has led a monthly poetry writing workshop since 1992. His poems have been published in anthologies, including *Odes and Elegies – Eco-Poetry from the Texas Gulf Coast* (2020) and *Lone Star Poetry* (2023), and several publications, including the *San Antonio Express-News* and *Voices de la Luna*. His poem "At the Cardiac Clinic" is original to this publication.

LEE ROBINSON grew up in the Carolinas and practiced law in Charleston for many years, where she was elected the first female president of the Charleston Bar Association. In 1998 she moved to Texas for a second marriage. For over ten years, she and her husband co-taught the course they designed, Medicine Through Literature, at the UT Health Science Center in San Antonio. She has published poems, stories and essays in many magazines and journals. Her first poetry collection, *Hearsay*, won the Poets Out Loud award from Fordham University Press. Her poem, "Winter," is original to this publication.

EDWIN ROMOND is the author of five books of poetry. His most recent, *Man at the Railing* (NYQ Books), won the 2022 Laura Boss Narrative Poetry Award. He has received fellowships from the

National Endowment for the Arts and from both the New Jersey and Pennsylvania State Councils on the Arts. His poem, "Champion," won the 2013 New Jersey Poetry Prize and Garrison Keillor has twice featured Romond's poetry on NPR's *The Writer's Almanac.* His poem "Waking" is from *Man at the Railing.*

SHEILA RONSEN is a poet and psychoanalyst living in New York City. She has been a regular participant in the annual San Miguel Poetry Week. Her work has appeared in *Main Street Rag, Poetica Magazine's Mizmor Anthology, POEM, The Avalon Literary Review,* and *Sin Fronteras.* She was shortlisted in the Hammond House International Poetry Prize in 2021. Her poem "No Parts Spared" is original to this publication.

GARY S. ROSIN is a Contributing Editor of *MacQueen's Quinterly.* His work has appeared in *Chaos Dive Reunion* (Mutabilis Press 2023), *Concho River Review, Sulphur River, Texas Poetry Calendar, Texas Poetry Assignment, The Ekphrastic Review,* and elsewhere. He has two chapbooks, *Standing Inside the Web* (Bear House Publishing 1990), and *Fire and Shadows* (Legal Studies Forum 2008). His poem "Senior Singles" is original to this publication.

JOHN RUTHERFORD is a poet living and writing in Beaumont, Texas. His work can be found in *Texas Poetry Assignment, The Basilisk Tree,* and *The Concho River Review.* His first chapbook, *Birds in a Storm* was published in 2023 by Naked Cat Publishing. His poem "Support" is original to this publication.

JAN SEALE is the 2012 Texas Poet Laureate and has held a fellowship in poetry with the National Endowment for the Arts. Her writing includes nine books of poetry, her latest being *Particulars: poems of smallness.* Forthcoming is a book of poems and photographs, *Border Biome,* reflecting where she lives in the Rio Grande Valley of Texas. Her poem "Playing the Flute after Long Absence" was previously published in *Texas Poetry Assignment.*

MOLLY SIZER is a retired rural sociologist living in southwest Oklahoma. She audits poetry classes from Professor John Morris at Cameron University in Lawton. She also volunteers her time and walks her miles at the nearby Wichita Mountains Wildlife Refuge, with 59,000 acres of protected public lands. She has read her work at Oklahoma's Scissortail Creative Writing Festival and with the Woody Poets. Some of her poems have been published in *Westview* and *The Oklahoma Review.* Her poem "At the Center" is original to this publication.

REILLY SMITH is a novice poet, a mother, and a graduate student of English at Lamar University. Her poem "The Chairs" was originally published in *Texas Poetry Assignment.*

BRADLEY R. STRAHAN taught poetry at Georgetown University for 12 years. From 2002-4 he was a Fulbright Professor of Poetry & American Culture in the Balkans. For over 40 years, he's been editor/publisher of *Visions-International.* He has 7 books of poetry & over 700 poems published in *America, Texas Observer, Confrontation, Christian Century, The Hollins Critic, Poet Lore*, and many anthologies. His poem "Reading Myself" is original to this publication.

SANDI STROMBERG's full-length poetry collection *Frogs Don't Sing Red* was released by Kelsay Books in 2023. Her work is widely published in literary journals and anthologies, most recently or forthcoming this spring in *Panoply, San Pedro River Review, synkroniciti, equinox, Pulse, The Windhover, formidable woman sanctuary,* and *The Orchards Poetry Journal.* She serves on the editorial staff of *The Ekphrastic Review.* Her poetry, translated into Dutch, has been published in the Netherlands in *Brabant Cultureel.* Her poem "Sixty Seconds of Infinity" was originally published in *Gyroscope Review.*

RICK SWANN is a member of Seattle's Greenwood Poets. His children's book *Our School Garden!* a series of linked poems about how community can grow from a garden, was awarded the Growing Good Kids Book Award from the American Horticultural Society. His poems have been accepted to *Windfall, Autumn Sky Poetry, Typehouse, English Journal,* and several other journals and anthologies. His poem "The Wish" is original to this publication.

LARRY D. THOMAS, the 2008 Texas Poet Laureate and a member of the Texas Institute of Letters, has published twenty-three print collections of poetry and numerous poetry chapbooks, both in print and online. Winner of the 2023 Spur Award from Western Writers of America (poetry category), he has also won two Western Heritage Wrangler Awards, two *Texas Review* Poetry Prizes, and the Violet Crown Book Award (poetry category) from the Writers' League of Texas. Thomas resides in the Chihuahuan Desert of southwestern New Mexico. His poem "Blueberry Picker" is original to this publication.

DAVID THOREEN's poems have appeared or are forthcoming in *Verse Daily, The American Journal of Poetry, Atlanta Review, The Comstock Review, Innisfree Poetry Journal, Kestrel, New Let-*

ters, *New Ohio Review, Presence, Seneca Review, Slate,* and else-where. He teaches writing and literature at Assumption University in Worcester, Massachusetts. His poem "Telemetry" originally appeared in *Innisfree Poetry Journal.*

ULIANA TRYLOWSKY lives in Beaumont, TX, and works at Lamar University as a Major Gifts Officer. Originally from Canada, she has lived in Texas for 25 years. Trylowsky moved to this area after working overseas in Ukraine and Georgia in the 1990s. She holds a B.A. in International Relations (University of British Columbia), and an M.A. in Soviet Studies (Carleton University). Trylowsky speaks Ukrainian, Russian, and French. Her poem "Aging Interrupted" is original to this publication.

PAT VALDATA is a poet and fiction writer. Her book *Where No Man Can Touch* won the 2015 Donald Justice Prize. A revised edition was published in June 2023 by Wind Canyon Books. Her work has also appeared in literary magazines including *Ecotone, Light, Little Patuxent Review, Loch Raven Review,* and *Valparaiso Poetry Review.* Her poem "Where the Time Goes" is original to this publication.

CLAIRE WEINER's work has been published in *After Hours Press, Burningwood Literary Review, Michigan Jewish History Society, Peninsula Poets,* and several others. She spent her non-writing career as a clinical social worker helping people make more sense of their life stories. She splits her time between Ann Arbor, and Tucson grateful to be in both places. Her poem "Penultimate Hospital Visit" is from *For a Chance to Walk on Streets of Gold,* her chapbook from Finishing Line Press.

LYNN WHITE lives in north Wales. Her poetry is influenced by issues of social justice, events, places, and people she has known or imagined. She is especially interested in exploring the boundaries of dream, fantasy, and reality. Her poem "Are We Any Older" first appeared in *Free Verse Revolution.*

A member of the Texas Institute of Letters, Albuquerque poet SCOTT WIGGERMAN is the author of three books of poetry, *Leaf and Beak: Sonnets, Presence,* and *Vegetables and Other Relationships*; and editor of several volumes, including *Wingbeats I & II: Exercises & Practice in Poetry,* and the brand-new anthology *Unknotting the Line: The Poetry in Prose.* He and writer David Meischen have run Dos Gatos Press for two decades, which published the *Texas Poetry Calendar* for most of its existence. In recent years, haiku and art have become more central to his work as an artist of both the page and canvas. Blame New Mexico. His poem "Skimming the Surface" originally appeared in *The Memory Palace: An Ekphrastic Anthology*.

JOHN WILLSON is a recipient of the Pushcart Prize and awards from the Academy of American Poets and the Artist Trust of Washington. His first full-length collection, *Call This Room a Station*, was published by MoonPath Press in 2020, and he was recently included in *Cascadia Field Guide: Art, Ecology, Poetry*. His poems have appeared in journals including *Bellevue Literary Review, Kyoto Journal, Northwest Review, Notre Dame Review, Sycamore Review*, and *Terrain.org*. John lives on Bainbridge Island, Washington, where he has been designated an Island Treasure for outstanding contributions to the arts. His poem "Pages from a Wall Calendar" first appeared in *Call This Room a Station*.

STEVE WILSON's poems have appeared in journals and anthologies nationwide and in six collections, the most recent entitled *Complicity* (2023). He lives in San Marcos, Texas. His poem "A Cascading, it is," first appeared in *Pulse: Voices from the Heart of Medicine*.

JERRY WINAKUR is a retired geriatrician and has previously published a memoir *Memory Lessons: A Doctor's Story*, (Hyperion, 2009), and a volume of poetry *Human Voices Wake Us* (Kent State U. Press, 2017.) For many years, he taught medical humanities and ethics at UTHealth-San Antonio. He is currently an Associate Editor of *Caring for the Ages* published by the Society for Post-Acute and Long-Term Care. His poem "Old Man Preps for Road Trip" is original to this publication.

CLARENCE WOLFSHOHL is a professor emeritus at William Woods University. Since his first publication in *The Road Apple Review*, he has been active in the small press as a writer and publisher for over fifty years, publishing poetry and non-fiction in many journals, both print and online, including *New Texas, San Pedro River Review, Agave, Cape Rock,* and *New Letters*. Among his publications are the e-chapbook *Scattering Ashes* (Virtual Artists Collective, 2016), *Queries and Wonderments* (El Grito del Lobo Press, 2017), and *Armadillos & Groundhogs* (2019). His poem "Dance of Oaks" originally appeared in the November 2018 *Red River Review*.

Editor

LAURENCE MUSGROVE is a professor of English at Angelo State University in San Angelo, Texas, where he teaches creative writing, literature, and composition from an applied Buddhist perspective. His verse collections include *Local Bird, The Bluebonnet Sutras*, and *A Stranger's Heart*, all from Lamar University Literary Press.